JOHN DEWEY

Twentieth-Century Political Thinkers
General Editors: Kenneth L. Deutsch and Jean Bethke Elshtain

Raymond Aron: The Recovery of the Political
  by Brian C. Anderson, American Enterprise Institute
Jacques Maritain: The Philosopher in Society
  by James V. Schall, Georgetown University
Martin Buber: The Hidden Dialogue
  by Dan Avnon, Hebrew University of Jerusalem
John Dewey: America's Philosopher of Democracy
  by David Fott, University of Nevada
Simone Weil: The Way of Justice as Compassion
  by Richard H. Bell, The College of Wooster
Gandhi: Struggling for Autonomy
  by Ronald J. Tercheck, University of Maryland at College Park

JOHN DEWEY

America's Philosopher of Democracy

DAVID FOTT

ROWMAN & LITTLEFIELD PUBLISHERS, INC.
Lanham • Boulder • New York • Oxford

ROWMAN & LITTLEFIELD PUBLISHERS, INC.

Published in the United States of America
by Rowman & Littlefield Publishers, Inc.
4720 Boston Way, Lanham, Maryland 20706

12 Hid's Copse Road
Cumnor Hill, Oxford OX2 9JJ, England

British Library Cataloguing in Publication Information Available

Library of Congress Cataloging-in-Publication Data
Fott, David, 1961–
    John Dewey : America's philosopher of democracy / David Fott.
      p.   cm.
    Includes bibliographical references and index.
    ISBN 0-8476-8759-7.—ISBN 0-8476-8760-0 (pbk.)
    1. Dewey, John, 1859–1952. I. Title.
  B945.D44F68   1998
  191—dc21   97-38482
                                          CIP

ISBN 0-8476-8759-7 (cloth : alk. paper)
ISBN 0-8476-8760-0 (pbk. : alk. paper)

Printed in the United States of America

♾ ™ The paper used in this publication meets the minimum requirements of
American National Standard for Information Sciences—Permanence of Paper
for Printed Library Materials, ANSI Z39.48—1984.

*To my parents, Solie and Mary Ready Fott,
with love and gratitude.*

CONTENTS

Acknowledgments   *ix*

1 Deweyan Pragmatism and Contemporary Political
   Thought   *1*

2 Dewey's Reformulation of Liberalism   *29*

3 Dewey's Justification of Democracy   *63*

4 Dewey's Aesthetics and Its Implications for Civic
   Education   *99*

5 On Dewey's and Socrates' Conceptions of Philosophy   *125*

Bibliography   *157*

Index   *163*

About the Author   *167*

ACKNOWLEDGMENTS

I owe much to several extraordinary teachers. At Clarksville High School in Tennessee, Grady and Kaye Warren taught me Latin and fostered a remarkable intellectual environment through their liberality. Dan Burden, who taught mathematics there, encouraged me to think for myself, despite the discomfort. At Vanderbilt University, Robert H. Birkby provided a lasting example of teaching spirit and methods. Alasdair MacIntyre led me to question the Enlightenment optimism that had ruled me until then.

This book began as my doctoral dissertation at Harvard University. There I had the great benefit of studying with Harvey C. Mansfield; I cannot thank him enough for his wisdom, support, and patience. On my committee Stephen Macedo and Dennis F. Thompson provided constructive criticism.

I am grateful for financial support provided during my graduate study by the Harry S. Truman Scholarship Foundation and the National Science Foundation.

Douglas Imig, Thomas Pangle, Bruce Pencek, David Steiner, Rick Tilman, David Welch, and Melissa Williams provided helpful conversation or comments on all or part of earlier drafts of the manuscript. The University of Nevada, Las Vegas, has been a productive place to work: I thank in particular the Center for Advanced Research under the direction of James Malek, Hart Wegner, and Guy Bailey successively; and graduate assistants Justin Cohen, Scott Hammond, Julene Haworth, Elaine Hernandez, Brent Parker, and Micki Winsett. The Department of Political Science at the University of Toronto kindly allowed me to work on revisions as a visiting scholar there. Dorothy Bradley and

Stephen Wrinn of Rowman & Littlefield have been a help in the process of publication.

Some of the material in this book originally appeared, in different form, in "John Dewey and the Philosophical Foundations of Democracy," *Social Science Journal* 28 (1991): 29–44. I acknowledge permission to use this material from JAI Press, Inc. Selections from *The Collected Works of John Dewey, 1882–1953* are copyright © 1969–91 by the Center for Dewey Studies, Southern Illinois University, reprinted by permission of the publisher. Any scholar of Dewey is in debt to the staff of that center—especially the general editor, Jo Ann Boydston—for the massive undertaking of publishing the standard edition of Dewey's writings.

1

DEWEYAN PRAGMATISM AND CONTEMPORARY POLITICAL THOUGHT

A critical study of the works of John Dewey can help us to see, and to undertake, a distinctively American way of life. Whether Dewey is a quintessentially American thinker or a thinker at odds with American moral, educational, and political principles is a question debated during his life and still today—and reasonably so. If, however, we may take the Declaration of Independence as at least a beginning point for a statement of fundamental American principles, Dewey seeks both to challenge and to uphold those principles. Indeed he tries to accomplish the same goal as Thomas Jefferson, who, in understanding and defining what makes an American, had to transcend Americanism. As long as one maintains respect for American political institutions, what higher American way of life could be imagined?

Thus it is no less true that a study of Dewey may help us to explore questions of import to human beings as human beings. Evidence that Dewey's thought offers a searching exploration of important questions is suggested by the number of recent books influenced, directly or indirectly, by him. Richard Rorty, Cornel West, Hilary Putnam, Charles Anderson, and John Patrick Diggins have written noteworthy books and articles endorsing or criticizing versions of pragmatism—or at least purported versions of pragmatism.[1] If Dewey is "America's philosopher of democracy," we may begin to examine Dewey's philosophy by examining its effects in the thoughts of some of those he influenced. Consideration of two central questions or issues raised by those authors will show why a close examination of Deweyan pragmatism can be beneficial and will help to pose questions important to that examination. The first of those questions is: What sort of philosophical justification may be found for liberal democracy as a form of government? The second is: Where is the proper distinction to be drawn between public and private in a liberal democracy?

Before we consider those two questions, it may first be helpful to explain what I mean by "Deweyan pragmatism." To give a full, clear account of pragmatism in general would be to write a book in itself—a book that I do not intend to write here. To offer a brief account of Deweyan pragmatism at the beginning of the book may give the appearance of arbitrariness. But to fail to offer, at the outset, any definition of my subject might be to invite misunderstanding. I believe that I may fairly solve that problem by invoking the work of two highly respected scholars in the field. First I quote from H.S. Thayer's critical history of pragmatism: Pragmatism is

> a theory of knowledge, experience, and reality maintaining . . . that thought and knowledge are biologically and socially evolved modes of adaptation to and control over experience and reality; . . . that all knowledge is evaluative of future experience and that thinking functions experimentally in anticipations of future experiences and consequences of actions—thus in organizing conditions of future observations and experience. Thought is a behavioral process manifested in controlled actualizations of selected, anticipated, and planned possibilities of future experience. . . . [T]heorizing over experience is, as a whole and in detail, fundamentally motivated and justified by conditions of efficacy and utility in serving our various aims and needs. . . . [A]side from esthetic and intrinsic interests, all theorizing is subject to the critical objective of maximum usefulness in serving our needs.[2]

What pragmatism opposes is a theory of truth as the static correspondence of idea and object. If truth were such static correspondence, we would need to transcend our idea in order to judge the degree of correspondence of idea to object. Such a theory of truth would provide no way to verify an idea.[3]

Second, as John E. Smith observes, Dewey in particular attacks the view that coming to know the truth entails correspondence of mind to "antecedent reality." Dewey's "defence of problem-solving as the transformation of an indeterminate or problematic situation into a determinate or reconstituted state of affairs, clearly placed himself outside the conform [i.e., correspondence] type."[4] Dewey is especially opposed to the passivity of the correspondence theory of truth. "[A]s Dewey points out, in the operation of inquiry various features of the situation and its elements are selected and modified; certain traits become of heightened significance, others are relegated to the background in their bearing, accordingly, in utility and relevance for the developing inquiry. The anticipation of new data and observations, and the introduction of activities of observation and experiment, since these are existential operations, 'modify the prior existential situation.' "[5] Thus Dewey prefers to call his pragmatism by the name "experimentalism," because the term "pragmatism" gives the misleading sense that all thought is for the sake of action, instead of for the sake of resolution of a problematic situation or unproblematic experience. I can say now that for Dewey the paradigmatic form of meaningful experience is aesthetic experience; but I defer further exposition along this line until chapter 4.

PHILOSOPHICAL JUSTIFICATION OF LIBERAL DEMOCRACY

Many contemporary academic philosophers and political theorists doubt that the principles of liberal democracy have a validity that transcends time and place. The last few decades have seen a revolt against the analytic philosophy that formerly dominated professional departments of philosophy, with its scientifically inspired project of solving philosophical problems once and for all through precise analysis of language. Among the leaders of that revolt is Rorty, who has criticized analytic philosophy for its commitment to "the construction of a permanent, neutral framework for inquiry, and thus for all of culture."[6] Rorty rejects the notion that there are "nonhistorical conditions of any possible historical development"; he rejects the "attempt to escape from history."[7] That revolt has taken the name "postmodernism," where postmodernism is usually defined, in the words of another of its leading figures, Jean-Francois Lyotard, as "incredulity toward metanarratives": disbelief in any grand theory that would uphold our moral and political practices.[8] Since Dewey's death, no one has done more to foster interest in him than Rorty (although his own claim to be a pragmatist or neopragmatist is questionable). In his influential *Philosophy and the Mirror of Nature* Rorty identified Dewey, Martin Heidegger, and Ludwig Wittgenstein as the three "most important" philosophers of this century.[9] More recently Rorty has said that Dewey has "eclipsed" the other two in importance.[10] Once we have set aside "the idea of ahistorical moral truth in the insouciant way that Dewey recommended," Rorty says, we shall understand that the members of our community are the only ones to whom we need to justify our beliefs and actions.[11] Liberal democracy is justified simply because our community considers it so. "For pragmatist social theory," he claims, "the question of whether justifiability to the community with which we identify entails truth is simply irrelevant."[12] While liberal democracy "may need philosophical articulation, it does not need philosophical backup."[13] Instead of engaging in a quest for justification of itself and its policies, Rorty's "liberal utopia" would settle for "narratives which connect the present with the past, on the one hand, and with utopian futures, on the other. More important, it would regard the realization of utopias, and the envisaging of still further utopias, as an endless process—an endless, proliferating realization of Freedom, rather than a convergence toward an already existing Truth."[14]

The evident charge to be leveled against Rorty's views is that, since they are relativistic and based on "a pragmatist theory about truth"—even a theory that "says that truth is not the sort of thing one should expect to have a philosophically interesting theory about"—they are meant to be stated as a theoretical position; and that, when stated as such, they are self-refuting.[15] How can Rorty avoid putting his thoughts forward as a timelessly true rejection of all timeless truth?

Rorty's first reply to this accusation was a denial that he is a relativist. Relativism is "the view that every belief on a certain topic, or perhaps about *any* topic, is as good as every other. No one holds this view."[16] If he held this view, Rorty suggested, he could be refuted with the argument noted above. "But such neat little dialectical strategies only work against lightly-sketched fictional characters."[17]

Yet more recently Rorty has acknowledged the force of the self-referential argument against his position. In *Contingency, Irony, and Solidarity* he turns away from an attempt to redefine or redescribe relativism and toward an attempt to grapple with the philosophic issue.[18] He realizes that he is engaged in advocating "irony"—a person's affirmation of his most central beliefs and desires while recognizing their historical contingency—on a theoretical level, and that he must "overcome authority without claiming authority."[19] The solution, he suggests, is to be found in simply forgetting that the problem exists. He points to Jacques Derrida, who "privatizes his philosophical thinking, and thereby breaks down the tension between ironism and theorizing. He simply drops theory—the attempt to see his predecessors steadily and whole—in favor of fantasizing about those predecessors, playing with them, giving free rein to the trains of association they produce."[20] Rorty concludes,

> Falling back on private fantasy is the only solution to the self-referential problem which such theorizing encounters, the problem of how to distance one's predecessors without doing exactly what one has repudiated them for doing. So I take Derrida's importance to lie in his having had the courage to give up the attempt to unite the private and the public, to stop trying to bring together a quest for private autonomy and an attempt at public resonance and utility. He privatizes the sublime, having learned from the fate of his predecessors that the public can never be more than beautiful.[21]

Thus theorizing ends in the abandonment of theory. The attempt to see "steadily and whole"—a prerequisite, one might say, to obtaining a view of the whole (if such a view is possible)—is left behind in favor of free association of ideas and images.

The obvious objection to this move on Rorty's part is that the theoretical implications, and thus the self-referential problem, do not evaporate when someone engages in flights of fancy. One need not believe in a Platonic theory of forms in order to make that objection. Rorty's reply, I believe, would be to ask what moral constraint could be invoked to suggest why he should not fantasize. Rorty thus endorses Wittgenstein's comment, "The way to solve the problem you see in life is to live in a way that will make what is problematic disappear."[22] But is solving a philosophical problem so simple?

In a similar vein to Rorty's, Cornel West has written a book the title of which praises "the American evasion of philosophy." By "the evasion of philosophy" he means the attempt to avoid metaphysical justifications of our moral and political practices. Dewey is one of West's heroes because he views Dewey as a major participant, albeit an ambivalent one, in the evasion.[23] In place of philosophy so construed, West wants to substitute a "prophetic pragmatism" that is a combination of "left romanticism" and Christianity.[24] Left romanticism is "the preoccupation with Promethean human powers, the recognition of the contingency of the self and society, and the audacious projection of desires and hopes in the form of regulative emancipatory ideals for which one lives and dies."[25] According to West, manifestation of this romanticism has occurred in three "waves": the American and French Revolutions, and the thought of Jefferson and Rousseau; dissatisfaction with the revolution, as seen in Emerson and Marx; and dissatisfaction with "Marxist-Leninism and Americanism," exemplified in the work of Roberto Unger.[26] West cites Unger's work approvingly as "an emancipatory experimentalism that promotes permanent social transformation and perennial self-development for the purposes of ever-increasing democracy and individual freedom. Yet, in contrast to most significant social thinkers, Unger is motivated by explicit religious concerns, such as a kinship with nature as seen in romantic love, or transcendence of nature as manifest in the hope for eternal life."[27]

This concern of Unger's, as well as West's emphasis on the sense of "tragedy" of human life, takes us to the other element of West's pragmatism, Christianity. For while left romanticism stresses political engagement, it cannot hope to eliminate all evil; therein lies the tragedy. Therein also lies the shortcoming of pragmatism, West says, because in Dewey's thought there is no sense of unavoidable evil. Yet, according to West, prophetic pragmatism remains romantic in that "it holds many experiences of evil to be neither inevitable nor necessary but rather the results of human agency, i.e., choices and actions."[28] Those experiences of evil are largely the result of unresolved socioeconomic conflicts; pragmatism cannot fully comprehend them because of its "inadequate grasp of the complex operations of power," which in turn is due to its "reluctance to take traditions of historical sociology and social theory seriously."[29]

West makes it clear that he shares the historicism of thinkers like Rorty.[30] The question follows: how can West hope to combine historicism with Christianity in one mixture, when Christianity asserts that humans have access to ahistorical, divine truth through the communication of that ahistorical truth in history? Moreover, West is unclear as to whether he accepts the theological heart of Christian teaching: on the same page he affirms both a Christianity "stripped of static dogmas and decrepit doctrines" and the truth of the Christian gospel.[31] The reader is left wondering what dogmas and doctrines West has in mind, although in a later writing West appears to indicate no support for any Christian dogma—short, perhaps, of the existence of God, because (I speculate here) rejection of that doctrine would be so hostile to "the rich, though flawed, traditions of Judaism and Christianity" that it might lead to "despair," which is one of "the major foes to be contested."[32] Yet "dogmatism" (along with "oppression") is given as another main foe to be contested.

Despite their differences, the moral conventionalism of Rorty and romanticism of West agree in rejecting any ahistorical justification of liberal democracy. Their views are based on an epistemological skepticism about our ability to know what is true or good about the world by nature. We cannot be sure that our words refer to anything real, Derrida and Rorty say; thus they speak of "the loss of the world." Hilary Putnam believes that such postmodernism cannot help us to find a philosophical middle way between moral absolutism, which Putnam finds indefensible in any version, and total moral relativism or skepticism: "[T]elling us again and again that 'there is nothing outside the text,' or that all our thought is simply 'marks and noises' which we are 'caused' to produce by a blind material world to which we cannot so much as *refer,* is not an exploration of any of them, but a fruitless oscillation between a linguistic idealism which is largely a fashionable 'put on' and a self-refuting scientism."[33] This deconstructionism is also politically irresponsible, for to say that reason is repressive—as at least Derrida does—encourages a dangerous extremism of left or right.[34]

Given this felt need to find a middle way, Putnam in his recent writings has turned toward pragmatism for inspiration, toward Dewey and William James. Putnam sees hope in their common conviction that "the solution to the problem of 'loss of the world' is to be found in action and not in metaphysics (or 'postmodern' anti-metaphysics, either)"; he seems to champion their claim (which he traces back to Kant) for the "primacy of practical reason."[35] He praises James's "holism": his "vision of fact, theory, value, and interpretation as all interdependent."[36] He lauds Dewey's *"normative"* conception of science: his view that scientific method involves cooperation and respect for the autonomy of the inquirer, and that it involves not value-free algorithms but maxims that require value-laden contextual interpretation.[37] Putnam's book *Rea-*

son, Truth and History previously sketched such a view, according to which our notion of truth presupposes a prior theory of rationality, which in turn presupposes our theory of the good.[38] This sounds relativistic, but Putnam insists that we must not lapse into relativism or skepticism, ultimately because no one can live in a consistently relativist way: we consider some moral judgments better than others because "that is the way that we . . . talk and think, and also the way that we are going to go on talking and thinking."[39]

Putnam operates with the premise that the only criterion for what is a fact is what it is rational to accept; but a statement can be rationally acceptable at a given time without being true. On this view, truth is idealized rational acceptability, independent of justification by any one person at any one moment—hence his support for Dewey's view of science—but not of all justification. Therefore, truth is a substantive, stable notion. By contrast, rational acceptability is relative to a person and one aspect of his theory of the good. This does not lead to subjectivism, however, because the fact that, say, coherence is considered an objective value enables our standards of rational acceptability to define our notion of objectivity. The result is objectivity-for-us and not in an absolute sense, but Putnam claims that we can have only that sort of objectivity. Our belief in the worth of liberal democracy has that sort of objectivity, according to Putnam's view.

He admits that his view appears to have trouble in dealing with the case of the Nazi whose view of what is reasonable is based on his own, quite different, firmly held theory of the good. If, as Putnam allows, most ethical values are subjective, how can we criticize the goals of the Nazi as irrational? His reply is as follows: If instead we focus on the Nazi's beliefs, we note that he will make assertions of Aryan supremacy and Jewish conspiracy, empirical claims that we can determine to be unfounded. We may then consider his goals irrational, because in pursuing them he is led to make unfounded claims.[40]

Dewey's view, according to Putnam, is that "some values are objectively relative—that is, rational *given the circumstances,* the nature and history, of those who make them."[41] This "objective relativism" "cannot handle the case of the Nazi," because it provides no way to say definitively that the Nazi's goals are wrong. "Objective relativism seems the *right* doctrine for many moral cases; but not for cases where rights and duties are manifest and sharp and the choice seems to us to be between right and wrong, good and evil."[42] Putnam faults Dewey's "bifurcation of goods into social goods, which are attained through the use of instrumental rationality, and consummatory experiences, which are ultimately aesthetic, [a bifurcation that] too closely resembles a similar positivist or empiricist division of life into the prediction and control of experiences and the enjoyment of experiences."[43] Because, according to Putnam, instrumental rationality accepts goals as given and speaks only to the efficiency of the means of achieving those goals, Dewey cannot refute the Nazi's claims. Yet Dewey does not accept goals as given, as we shall see in chapter 3.

Putnam's position is also a sort of "objective relativism": he maintains that some things are true and some things are reasonable, but we can say so only if we have a language, if we have a "language game"; and that "language game rests not on proof or on Reason but *trust*" in something.[44] It is trust, or faith, that underlies all of our use of language. What leads us to lapse into total relativism is an inability to "accept" or "acknowledge" the world or other people "without the guarantees" of metaphysical certainty that our "language game" is *the* true one.[45] Does this view best describe our situation?

Like Putnam, Charles Anderson also seems to want to find ground between moral absolutism and moral relativism. In his highly praised *Pragmatic Liberalism* Anderson aims to show how liberal political theory should be applied to practice. He wants to combine the schools of liberalism and pragmatism. "[P]ragmatism needs liberalism if it is not to become a vague and indeterminate counsel, perhaps, in the end, a doctrine of sheer expediency. . . . On the other hand, liberalism is empty and formal without pragmatic method. The abstract principles of liberalism require interpretation."[46]

Why complement pragmatism with liberalism, though, instead of with Marxism or fascism? Anderson's response to this question is unclear. At one point he writes, "In our society, liberal principles provide the normative structure for pragmatic method. Louis Hartz observed that pragmatism 'fed' on America's commitment to liberalism and suggested that 'It is only when you take your ethics for granted that all problems emerge as problems of technique.' "[47] This passage provides a conventionalist answer that seems to put Anderson in the camp of Rorty. Liberal principles are appropriate simply because they are our way of handling our affairs. Yet on the next page, explaining why liberalism needs interpretation, he remarks, "The great values of freedom, equality, justice, and social efficiency may be, in a certain sense, 'self-evident,' but what they mean when applied in diverse circumstances is not at all clear."[48] This passage is compatible with Jefferson's reliance on natural rights, although Anderson's talk of "values" is much vaguer than the "unalienable Rights" of the Declaration of Independence. Moreover, Anderson goes no further in explaining the sense in which the worth of freedom and equality (however they are defined) may be "self-evident."

Admittedly, it is not his stated purpose in the book to seek out or to provide a philosophical defense of liberalism. According to him, "It is not, in fact, the philosophic grounding, or the ordering, but the *application* of the fundamental principles that generates the great disputes of liberal politics."[49] Yet Anderson underestimates the relevance of disagreements about the ordering of the principles of liberalism, as well as disagreements about its philosophical foundation, to practical matters.[50]

As to whether pragmatism can provide moral and political guidance, John Patrick Diggins's *The Promise of Pragmatism* offers a more historical approach. Diggins's assessment of pragmatism is not a simple one. On the one hand, he suggests agreement with the rejection by pragmatism of indubitable foundations for our moral and political practices. In this respect too he endorses postmodernism.[51] But he devotes much effort to a sympathetic examination of the historian Henry Adams, who accused pragmatism of refusing to face the problem of the world's meaninglessness in an intellectually honest way: it is too optimistic that the union of science and political power will provide legitimate, constructive authority. Not only does Dewey fail to consistently apply his pragmatist principles to political affairs (he notes Dewey's opposition to American involvement in World War II on the basis of disillusionment with the results of World War I—that is, Dewey's unpragmatic failure to consider the world situation in the 1930s on its own terms), but Dewey's conviction about the fruitfulness of collective processes, scientific and political, is problematic: he merely "presupposes that a collectivized body politic is more enlightened and moral than its defective human parts, and that interest loses its egoistic character when it is directed toward public rather than private ends."[52]

But Diggins can find Dewey partially friendly to his "eleven theses on what we in American history always wanted to know until we came to realize that we already know it"—and we have known it, Diggins tells us, since the first New England Calvinists.[53] Those theses include the following: a rejection of the Enlightenment notion that reason provides a clear link between human mind and natural processes; a rejection of any absolute knowledge; a belief that humans nonetheless need absolute knowledge; hence the assumption that truth "can be found as an act of uncovering or recovering"; and a belief that "there is no essence" or foundation behind our mental and physical activity.

This is not to say that Diggins sees no important philosophical differences among American political thinkers—no differences between, say, the Calvinists and Richard Rorty. Nor is it to say that Diggins finds Rorty's writings unproblematic. Rorty wants to maintain a liberal democracy devoted to preventing (physical) cruelty and suffering in the world without appealing to transcendent standards of justice; Diggins doubts that he can do so. Moreover, in "turning toward language, discourse, and conversation, is not [Rorty's] neopragmatism under the illusion that philosophy can continue as a linguistic exercise and history can survive as a tale told by a narrator who admits to being unable to know the reality of past events?"[54] Yet Diggins finds as much philosophical kinship as dissimilarity between the postmodern rejection of philosophy as quest for foundations and the American founders' reliance on passion and interest as substitutes for reason to guide a polity.[55]

Diggins's book is ultimately frustrating because he does not face squarely the issue of historicism. As noted above, he claims that "the human subject is driven to assume that truth can be found as an act of uncovering or recovering because the rationalist mind presupposes the presence of what it is looking for (Heidegger) and treats as objective discovery what is actually imposed interpretation (Nietzsche)." In other words, he claims that Nietzsche and Heidegger *assume* the inadequacy of historicism as a philosophic position. It would be surprising if that claim did justice to either thinker. Elsewhere Diggins writes, "Historicism had made the modern mind aware that theory has no atemporal character of rational judgment. Rather it expresses the conventions, interests, and practices of a given situation and thus cannot attain the disinterested objectivity that would make it truthful instead of conditional. Such reasoning, *while perhaps epistemologically persuasive,* fails to consider nonphilosophical grounds for continuing the distinction between theory and practice."[56] Theory may be irreducible to practice because it claims "not to represent truth but to question it."[57] That passage puts in doubt not only Diggins's response to historicism but also the standard of his response to it: why would he fail to be guided by what is epistemologically persuasive?

The criticisms I have raised with the authors considered so far suggest an examination of Dewey's thought to see whether it is susceptible to the same difficulties. Four of the five authors I have mentioned here—Rorty, West, Putnam, and Diggins—directly raise the question of the relation between Deweyan pragmatism and postmodernism; and the fifth author, Anderson, indirectly raises the question whether Deweyan pragmatism is closer to the natural rights thinking of the Declaration of Independence or to moral conventionalism. As we have seen, these authors encourage us to ask the following questions, all related to the central issue of the justification of democracy: Does Dewey seek philosophical "backup" for democratic government or merely philosophical "articulation"? Is Dewey, famously opposed to philosophical absolutisms, nonetheless closer to Jefferson than to Rorty? Does Dewey seek to escape self-refuting relativism through anything like Derridean fantasizing or romanticism? Does Dewey face squarely the matter of historicism?

PUBLIC AND PRIVATE IN LIBERAL DEMOCRACY

The second central issue involved in recent works about pragmatism that I shall consider here is the distinction between public and private in political theory. Rorty attempts to put Dewey to work in the service of a "postmodernist bourgeois liberalism."[58] The public aspect of this liberal democracy consists of citizens "who think that cruelty is the worst thing we do."[59] The purpose of liberal society is only "to make life easier for poets and revolutionaries while seeing to it that they make life harder for others only by words, and not deeds."[60] "J.S. Mill's suggestion that governments devote themselves to optimizing the balance between leaving people's private lives alone and preventing suffering seems to me pretty much the last word."[61]

Mill is well known as a defender of free speech. Yet, unlike Mill's, Rorty's political society is not one that provides an arena for the free exchange of views among people with differing fundamental outlooks on life; indeed he has a very restrictive notion of acceptable public discourse. Regarding discussions of public policy, he claims that "when the individual finds in her conscience beliefs that are relevant to public policy but incapable of defense on the basis of beliefs common to her fellow citizens, she must sacrifice her conscience on the altar of public expediency."[62] Broad, controversial philosophical questions have no place in politics. "A liberal democracy will not only exempt opinions on such matters from legal coercion, but also aim at disengaging discussions of such questions from discussions of social policy."[63] It will leave them to be settled in private, where Nietzschean self-creation is the ideal. Our public activity can have no justification beyond convention.

To say that Rorty offers us "the politics of insouciance" may appear a strange charge to level at one who claims that the purpose of politics is the prevention of cruelty. Rorty does not differ here from the liberal tradition beginning with Thomas Hobbes, who would never be accused of such. Where he does differ, however, is in his attempt to decouple controversial philosophical questions—and religion altogether—from politics. The separation of church from state serves liberal politics (as well as the church) by putting a limit on its reach over citizens' lives and moderating conflict. But we may ask whether the complete separation of religion from politics, advocated by many today in addition to Rorty, works to deprive liberal politics of gravity. The conviction that politics involves not just mundane matters, but also to some degree ultimate questions of human existence—even if the purpose of politics is not to solve those questions—may have an ennobling effect on politics that would be lost if Rorty's plan to forget about such questions were adopted. Without that ennobling effect, is it not likely that liberal politics would eventually lose sight of its serious goals of preventing cruelty and providing space for private activity? Rorty's advocacy of "fantasizing" as the model private activity may make it even more difficult to maintain the requisite level of seriousness in the public sphere.

The distinction between public and private is also treated in Anderson's book. As we have seen, Anderson refers to the "empty and formal" character of liberalism as justifying the need for pragmatism. Yet, I would argue, the formal character of liberalism makes the compatibility and value of pragmatism at least initially suspect. Liberalism is formal in two senses: it requires government to operate through certain specified forms in order to achieve its ends, including the protection of individual liberties; and it leaves the use of those liberties to be determined privately by individuals. Today we rarely question the value of the second sense of formality (although Anderson himself does, as I shall explain); but the formality of liberalism in the first sense is threatened whenever and wherever the means that are used to attain a certain end violate requirements of the system—a not uncommon occurrence in American history.[64]

The value of pragmatism as it relates to each of these two senses of formality is questionable. First, it cannot prescribe to an individual how to use his liberties; as Anderson claims, pragmatism must take its own goals from an outside source. Second, it encourages continual questioning of, rather than deep respect for, constitutional forms. To anticipate our examination of Dewey, Dewey says that universal suffrage and frequent elections are not sacred but are to be judged according to their contribution to the broader democratic ideal.[65] Sanctity in a religious sense may or may not be the quality for which we should be looking in constitutional forms; but it is certainly debatable whether Dewey does enough to encourage stability, if he is willing to reconsider as basic a form as universal suffrage.

Dewey's brand of liberalism has often been criticized for collectivist tendencies, and the same charge may be made against Anderson's pragmatic liberalism. Anderson claims that the performance of functional associations in civil society is a matter of public concern. His choice of examples to illustrate the point is noteworthy. Although in general a private club should be able to determine its own members, nevertheless "when that club is understood as a forum for business and civic discussion, the situation changes, and discrimination on grounds of race or sex becomes a public concern. Equality trumps liberty, *because* of the purpose of the enterprise concerned."[66]

Thus, according to Anderson, a number of individuals may not form an association for the purpose of discussion of public affairs and legally discriminate in selection of members on the basis of race or sex. Leaving aside the question whether such discrimination would ever be morally virtuous, we may ask whether the government should guarantee access for all to the organization (if we assume that the organization receives no special support from the government). Does the purpose of the organization outweigh the members' desire to determine their own associates—particularly since many different kinds of groups have as a purpose the discussion of public affairs, and a person who is excluded from one group may become a member of another?

Anderson's reasoning here is disturbing for the threat it poses to the relative independence of civil society from governmental interference. The political theory of classical liberalism, as Anderson observes, recognizes certain matters as fundamentally private and outside the public sphere; he goes so far as to say that on this view each area of life has its own rationality.[67] Now certainly no matter is completely outside the public sphere: religious practices, for example, must stay within publicly reasonable limits. Yet the difference between classical liberalism and Anderson's view is significant. In contrast to classical liberalism, pragmatic liberalism is first and foremost "a theory of practical political reason that applies not only to the state but to all forms of organized human endeavor."[68] No distinction between private and public can be of much use, then, for any purpose is potentially a public one.

In this respect Anderson follows Dewey, who teaches, "The line of demarcation [between private and public] . . . has to be discovered experimentally."[69] Neither Dewey nor Anderson wants the totalitarian conclusions to which pragmatic liberalism might lead, but perhaps neither can preclude them as long as one method—for Dewey, "the method of intelligence," for Anderson, a single rationality to replace the differing rationalities of the separate spheres of life—is imposed on all organized human activity. The question deserves further study, which I shall give it in chapter 2.

West's "left romanticism" should also be mentioned here. As we have seen, West cites Unger's work approvingly as "an emancipatory experimentalism that promotes permanent social transformation and perennial self-development for the purposes of ever-increasing democracy and individual freedom." It is safe to say that someone who has shown the concern of West in matters of civil rights, particularly in matters of race, does not want to espouse a teaching that leads to totalitarianism any more than does Anderson. But West should not be surprised if his teaching led to that conclusion, especially since he trusts that Christian morals can be preserved without their theological foundations—a questionable trust indeed.[70]

In connection with the question of public and private it is also worth noting the role that Dewey has begun to play in the discussions between those who emphasize the individual rights of liberalism and those who complain that liberalism per se does not allow for an adequate sense of community. Michael Sandel notes favorably what he calls Dewey's "communitarian liberalism": "For Dewey, the primary problem with American democracy in his day was not an insufficient emphasis on justice and rights, but the impoverished character of public life."[71] Sandel observes that Dewey's liberalism and a rights-based liberalism may not differ very much in practice, but at least Dewey maintains the ideal of "a national community" with "public deliberation."[72] But is this true? Can Dewey be fairly characterized as communitarian, and, if so, what sort of communitarian? I shall address those questions also in chapter 2.

In initially raising the two main questions above—What justification is available for liberal democracy? What is the proper distinction between public and private in liberal democracy?—as well as the related questions I have also raised, I do not want to distort Dewey by asking him questions that he does not attempt to answer, to attempt to view Dewey through "eyes" that impose concerns of their own while failing to notice his concerns. But the questions I raise in this introduction are Dewey's concerns. Moreover, answers to those questions will emerge from an examination of Dewey's thought on its own terms, if also in comparison and contrast with the work of other major political thinkers.

SCHOLARLY CONTEXT OF THIS BOOK

Scholarship on Dewey has expanded quite a bit in the last two decades, but studies of his political theory are still few and far between. Alfonso Damico's relatively early study focuses on the relation between the individual human being and the community; it rightly sees Dewey's vision of the good life as radically opposed to any separation between individual and community, or between freedom and authority. But Damico does not trace that opposition to Dewey's principle of existential continuity between humans and their environment, as I shall show. Instead Damico stops short by saying, "Dewey's defense of democratic methods must and can stand on the worth of those methods apart from any appeal to scientific methodology."[73] This neglects that for Dewey democracy as a way of life depends on his faith in scientific method, as I shall also show.

My treatment of Dewey differs as well from Steven Rockefeller's book on Dewey's religion. Rockefeller wants to resurrect the Dewey who wrote *A Common Faith,* his major work on religion. According to Rockefeller, "Dewey's philosophical quest was founded upon a religious faith. This faith was a faith in intelligence in the broad sense indicated, that is, a faith not only in human reason but also a faith in God as the Divine Reason and the ground of organic unity, of the intelligibility and meaningfulness of all existence."[74] Dewey "would always consider to be divine whatever unified the ideal and the actual and created organic unity. . . . The unification of self, of society, and of self and world became for him vitally important religious values."[75] To a large extent what Rockefeller says of Dewey is an accurate description of his thought; but Rockefeller does not give sufficient emphasis to Dewey's protestations that no special philosophical significance should be attached to his use of the word "God" to characterize the unifying of actual and ideal.[76] With that in mind, Rockefeller's use of "Divine Reason"—especially the capital letters—cannot be suitable: it indicates that he is more satisfied with Dewey's "common faith" than was Dewey himself. When Rockefeller writes that "Dewey also associates religious experience with an attitude of piety toward nature and with mystical intuitions of oneness with the larger whole which is the universe," he endorses mysticism to a greater extent than Dewey intends to do.[77] There has been, and continues to be, much room for debate about the relation between philosophy and religion; but Rockefeller refuses either openly to embrace any traditional religious doctrines or to seek a nonreligious basis for philosophizing (admittedly, the latter alternative does not necessarily lead one away from religion), and he does not really break new ground on the subject.

Robert Westbrook has written a very thorough intellectual biography of Dewey, the main point of which is to explain Dewey as "a minority, not a majority, spokesman within the liberal community, a social philosopher whose democratic vision failed to find a secure place in liberal ideology—in short, a more radical voice than has been generally assumed."[78] I think that he makes that point successfully, while he recognizes that Dewey's support for participatory democracy stopped short of a condemnation of representative democracy. Westbrook provides a comprehensive account of Dewey's works. He outlines certain differences between Dewey and Rorty, I believe correctly as far as he goes, although like Damico he does not trace Dewey's defense of democracy to its philosophical roots in order to show the full difference between Deweyan pragmatism and postmodernism.[79]

Alan Ryan's recent book on Dewey works from much the same political perspective as Westbrook's, with more attention to both the historical context and the philosophical issues, but less attention to the details of Dewey's writings. Ryan considers Dewey to have been "very nearly successful" in his attempt "to unite the religious conviction that the world is a *meaningful* unity with a secular twentieth-century faith in the scientific analysis of both nature and humanity."[80] At certain places in this book Ryan's interpretation errs: For example, he says that Dewey's "instrumentalism" holds that "all thought was for the sake of action."[81] That is a standard misinterpretation of pragmatism; Dewey clearly did not believe that, and the misinterpretation was one reason why he objected to use of the term "pragmatism" to describe his philosophy, as Ryan himself realizes a few lines following that quotation.

Ryan also makes the more controversial claim that "Dewey's hostility to absolutisms was thoroughgoing, and he knew better than to make pragmatism's commitment to experiment an absolute."[82] Yet he undercuts his own claim only eight pages later by writing, "To the extent that Dewey held any ideal as an absolute, he was absolutely committed to not abandoning his fellow citizens as irredeemably irrational, gullible, and shortsighted and absolutely committed to not using philosophy as a consolation."[83] This passage shows that Ryan is not so sure about Dewey's opposition to absolutism, and that we are in need of more rigorous thought concerning absolutisms and the possibility and desirability of avoiding them. If Ryan is wrong and Dewey is ultimately an absolutist of some sort, then he may also be wrong that Dewey did not use philosophy as a consolation.

Ryan observes in general that an intimate connection exists between Dewey's metaphysics and his social and political theory; but he does not specifically articulate that link.[84] That such a link exists would make Dewey appear less of a postmodernist than Rorty claims. But Ryan agrees with Rorty that it makes sense to view Dewey, Heidegger, and Wittgenstein as cut from the same philosophical cloth: Rorty's claim is "surprisingly plausible. It is at least true that all three rejected the idea that philosophy was in the business of providing foundations for knowledge, art, morality, or politics."[85] That is a highly disputable assertion as it concerns Dewey. Moreover, it apparently contradicts two of Ryan's earlier statements that Dewey's philosophy contains unity and system.[86]

That Dewey may have enjoyed some success in his philosophical project does not prevent Ryan from finding significant failures. First and most important, Dewey's political theory, in its opposition to any radical separation between the individual and the community, neglects to allow any room for private life. "It is hard to repress the thought that Dewey may simply have been asking too much of democratic politics and that a moderate degree of alienation from one another is the price we pay for a liberal society and its virtues of privacy and diversity."[87] For example, Dewey "had nothing to say about sex."[88] "The individual in Dewey always seems to be going outward into the world; 'the bliss of solitude' is not a Deweyan thought. . . . [O]ne result of this lack of interest in the private, the intimate, and the sexually charged is that family life gets shortchanged as well, and at a time when we are terribly puzzled about how to get the benefits of stable family life without unduly interfering with the pursuit of happiness, this is rather a loud silence."[89] Second, the lack of detail in Dewey's political theory "leaves us wondering whether his view of participatory democracy is that of the student insurgents of the 1960s or that of the Quaker meetinghouse and anyway not sure we can run a country of 280 million on either basis."[90] Dewey's call for a more participatory democracy "underestimated the obduracy of large institutions, as well as the unpredictability of institutional change."[91] Third, "the unclarity of his educational views leaves room for excesses: the reduction of work to mere play; the reduction of moral training to mere manipulation; the reduction of vocational education to job training for the untalented."[92] Ryan admits to "some sympathy" with Richard Hofstadter's view that Dewey's educational thought has contributed to the anti-intellectualism of American life.[93]

Thus Ryan concludes that "we must reject at least some of Dewey's moral and social vision, perhaps rather a lot. . . . We may also quarrel over the possibility of a wholly democratic culture," and Dewey's failure to distinguish high from low culture. "This does not threaten social democratic politics, though it may well alter our view of their value. . . . [W]e must be anxious about how to reconcile classlessness and high culture." But if a rejection of Dewey's moral and social vision lessens our estimation of social democratic politics, how could it not threaten social democratic politics?

Among recent books concerning Dewey, David Steiner's stands out as explaining more clearly than others do the connection between Dewey's political theory and his metaphysics. Steiner observes that Dewey's metaphysics is the foundation for his political theory. He also notes the foundational role of the principle of continuity in Dewey's thought; for Dewey democracy as a way of life is incompatible with a metaphysical dichotomy of mind and world.[94] But Steiner does not trace all of the steps along the way from Dewey's "naturalistic metaphysics" to his conception of democratic government. Moreover, the main point of his book is to argue for a particular conception of democratic politics as primarily citizens' judging of the rhetoric of their leaders. Is this also Dewey's conception of democratic politics?

Despite this renewal of scholarly interest, Dewey's writings (with the exception of his educational writings) have not received the attention that one would expect. During his life (and he died no longer ago than 1952) Dewey was frequently hailed as the greatest American philosopher ever to have lived. Perhaps part of the explanation for the neglect may be found in the course taken by academic departments of philosophy in the English-speaking world in the last several decades: Analytic philosophy, hostile to Dewey's pragmatism, became dominant even before his death. As a project of attempting to solve philosophical problems by arriving at precise meanings of words through linguistic analysis, it could have little interest in the writings of one who admitted that his work on his last book was "the first conscious, serious effort I *ever* made to get a firm terminology."[95]

But, as I suggested earlier, the possibility exists that through coming to understand Dewey twentieth-century Americans may come to see more clearly the implications of many of our own thoughts. Pragmatic ways of thought have been, and are, extremely influential in American life. Despite inattention to the writings of Dewey and other pragmatists, there is reason to believe the claim of James Nichols Jr. that "no alternative [school of thought] has come near to attaining pragmatism's status in American life."[96] That statement is quite strong when one considers the influence of the early modern view of natural law on the Declaration of Independence and so much American political thought. Dewey has exerted a strong and obvious influence in the field of education, an influence that subtly continues despite the attacks on his doctrines from many educational reformers.

Nevertheless, one must recognize two special obstacles to arriving at an understanding of Dewey. First, it is almost universally admitted that Dewey's books and articles do not make easy reading (a fact that may partially explain the neglect he has suffered). One must admit the obvious, that his prose is at least awkward, at most obscure. What is probably forever uncertain is the extent to which this unclarity is due to a deficient literary sensibility, or to an enduring thought on Dewey's part that he had a radical teaching to deliver that could not be expressed in traditional language—given the connotations of traditional terms— combined with an enduring uncertainty as to how to replace traditional terms.

The second obstacle to understanding Dewey is that his writings fall into a number of different categories: scholarly books and articles, articles for popular journals and magazines, reports of committees, letters, transcripts of public speeches. Much of the nonacademic writing is philosophical or semiphilosophical in nature. Late in his life he wrote to Arthur F. Bentley, coauthor of his final book, "I have used language *ad hoc* to try to get over a particular point to a given class of readers, without much respect for coherence in system."[97] This statement usefully reminds us to be aware of the audience a particular work is addressed to when we interpret it; but it also leads us to expect that we might find contradictions if we should try to extract a philosophical system from Dewey's writings.

That expectation should not cause us to lower our estimation of Dewey; for the same expectation would hold for Plato and Nietzsche, two great philosophers who were not builders of systems. Yet I believe and shall attempt to show that one may at least approach extracting a system from Dewey's writings without distorting their meaning. Thus I disagree with Sidney Hook's claim that Dewey "had no system in the traditional sense."[98] I also believe that Richard Bernstein concedes too much to Rorty's interpretation of Dewey—as, in Rorty's words, "therapeutic rather than constructive, edifying rather than systematic"—when he calls such an interpretation "true as far as it goes" (albeit simultaneously "a gross distortion").[99]

I do not mean to imply, however, that Dewey's philosophical views did not change over the course of his long career. In the two decades surrounding the turn of the century Dewey's thought made a gradual yet obvious shift away from Hegelian idealism and toward pragmatism. He made the break with idealism explicit in 1903 in *Studies in Logical Theory*. In this work I focus on Dewey's pragmatic period, with little attention to his thought before 1903.[100]

The rest of this book proceeds as follows: In chapter 2 I take up Dewey's reformulation of liberalism, examining Dewey's notion of "the public" as a possible liberal alternative to the traditional liberal notion of civil society, considering whether his liberal theory is able to avoid the dangers of the tyranny of public opinion noted by such thinkers as Alexis de Tocqueville. Thus I begin my direct engagement with Dewey by turning to the second of the two major questions I identified at the beginning of this chapter. I do so because it is easier to begin with the more concrete aspects of Dewey's political theory and move to the philosophical basis of that political theory. Chapter 3 explains Dewey's defense of democratic government and traces it to its metaphysical roots so as to illuminate Dewey's belief in democracy more fully than it has been before, and so as to rebut the widely noted interpretation of Dewey as opposed to all philosophical bases for politics.

Dewey's claim that any moral or political philosophy that "is not grounded in a comprehensive philosophy" is merely "a projection of arbitrary personal preference" clearly marks him as offering a more thoughtful approach than Rorty.[101] But is that claim correct? A solution to that question requires that we understand Dewey's comprehensive philosophy, to which his aesthetics is crucial. Chapter 4 considers Dewey's aesthetics and its implications for his political thought. By comparing and contrasting Dewey with other thinkers, I shall offer reasons why we could determine that Dewey's emphasis on creativity would not have undemocratic consequences. But I conclude by suggesting that there are reasons to fear that the centrality of creativity and art for his civic educational reflections would pose a hazard for democracy, and that his teaching lacks what is needed to forestall that hazard. I trace that difficulty to Dewey's problematic understanding of the relation between philosophy and science, which I examine in chapter 5 by comparing and contrasting Dewey's and Socrates' conceptions of philosophy. The latter appears to me a more promising, open-minded way to think about politics.

NOTES

1. In addition to works discussed in this chapter, a number of books on or involving pragmatism, written within the last decade or so, indicate a revival of pragmatist thought. Those works include the following: Larry A. Hickman, *John Dewey's Pragmatic Technology* (Bloomington: Indiana University Press, 1990); Timothy V. Kaufman-Osborn, *Politics/Sense/Experience: A Pragmatic Inquiry into the Promise of Democracy* (Ithaca: Cornell University Press, 1991); Joseph Margolis, *Pragmatism without Foundations: Reconciling Realism and Relativism* (Oxford: Basil Blackwell, 1986); C. G. Prado, *The Limits of Pragmatism* (Atlantic Highlands, N.J.: Humanities Press International, 1987); Eugene Rochberg-Halton, *Meaning and Modernity: Social Theory in the Pragmatic Attitude* (Chicago: University of Chicago Press, 1986); Sandra B. Rosenthal, *Speculative Pragmatism* (Amherst: University of Massachusetts Press, 1986).

2. H. S. Thayer, *Meaning and Action: A Critical History of Pragmatism*, 2d ed. (Indianapolis: Hackett, 1981), 431.

3. Ibid., 124.

4. John E. Smith, *Purpose and Thought: The Meaning of Pragmatism* (Chicago: University of Chicago Press, 1978), 76.

5. Thayer, *Meaning and Action*, 199.

6. Richard Rorty, *Philosophy and the Mirror of Nature* (Princeton: Princeton University Press, 1979), 8.

7. Ibid., 9.

8. Jean-Francois Lyotard, *The Postmodern Condition: A Report on Knowledge,* trans. Geoff Bennington and Brian Massumi (Minneapolis: University of Minnesota Press, 1984), xxiv.

9. Rorty, *Philosophy and Mirror*, 5.

10. Richard Rorty, *Objectivity, Relativism, and Truth*, Philosophical Papers, vol. 1 (Cambridge: Cambridge University Press, 1991), 16.

11. Richard Rorty, "The Priority of Democracy to Philosophy," in *The Virginia Statute for Religious Freedom: Its Evolution and Consequences in American History,* ed. Merrill D. Peterson and Robert C. Vaughan (Cambridge: Cambridge University Press, 1988), 259.

12. Ibid.

13. Ibid., 260.

14. Richard Rorty, *Contingency, Irony, and Solidarity* (Cambridge: Cambridge University Press, 1989), xvi.

15. Richard Rorty, *Consequences of Pragmatism* (Minneapolis: University of Minnesota Press, 1982), xiii.

16. Ibid., 166.

17. Ibid., 167.

18. See Rorty, *Contingency, Irony, and Solidarity,* 7–8, 104–5, 125.

19. Ibid., 105.

20. Ibid., 125.

21. Ibid.

22. Ludwig Wittgenstein, *Culture and Value* (Oxford: Basil Blackwell, 1980), 27e; quoted in Richard J. Bernstein, *Beyond Objectivism and Relativism: Science, Hermeneutics, and Praxis* (Oxford: Basil Blackwell, 1983), xv.

23. West agrees with Rorty, saying that Deweyan pragmatists take "a more insouciant attitude toward truth" than pragmatists influenced by C. S. Peirce. Cornel West, "The Limits of Neopragmatism," in *Pragmatism in Law and Society,* ed. Michael Brint and William Weaver (Boulder, Colo.: Westview, 1991), 122.

24. West avers that prophetic pragmatism does not require a religious basis or component, but his own version has one.

25. Cornel West, *The American Evasion of Philosophy: A Genealogy of Pragmatism* (Madison: University of Wisconsin Press, 1989), 215.

26. Ibid., 215–18.

27. Ibid., 214.

28. Ibid., 228.

29. West, "Limits of Neopragmatism," 121.

30. Ibid.

31. West, *American Evasion of Philosophy,* 233.

32. West, "Limits of Neopragmatism," 124, 125.

33. Hilary Putnam, *Pragmatism* (Oxford: Blackwell, 1995), 75. Putnam's first quotation is a saying of Derrida's; his second quotation is from Rorty, conference in Paris sponsored by College Internationale de Philosophie, 3 May 1990.

34. Hilary Putnam, *Renewing Philosophy* (Cambridge: Harvard University Press, 1992), 132–33. Yet Putnam also rejects the view of truth as correspondence between mental image and object in world, "the spectator theory" (see, e.g., Putnam, *Pragmatism,* 30).

35. Putnam, *Pragmatism,* 74, 42.

36. Ibid., 19.

37. Ibid., 72 (italics in original). See also generally 70–74.

38. Hilary Putnam, *Reason, Truth and History* (Cambridge: Cambridge University Press, 1981), 215.

39. Putnam, *Renewing Philosophy,* 135.

40. Putnam, *Reason, Truth and History,* 212–13.

41. Ibid., 167.

42. Ibid., 168.

43. Hilary Putnam, "A Reconsideration of Deweyan Democracy," in *Pragmatism in Law and Society,* ed. Brint and Weaver, 238; originally published in *Southern California Law Review* 63 (summer 1990): 1671–97.

44. Putnam, *Renewing Philosophy,* 177.
45. Ibid., 178.
46. Charles W. Anderson, *Pragmatic Liberalism* (Chicago: University of Chicago Press, 1990), 2–3.
47. Ibid., 2. The quotation is from Louis Hartz, *The Liberal Tradition in America* (New York: Harcourt, 1955), 19.
48. Anderson, *Pragmatic Liberalism,* 3.
49. Ibid.
50. To take one example, John Rawls has tried to articulate the two principles of justice that are fundamental to liberal democracies. The first principle provides for the equal right of all people to basic liberties; the second principle stipulates limits on the acceptable level of social and economic inequality. See John Rawls, *A Theory of Justice* (Cambridge: Harvard University Press, Belknap Press, 1971), 302. Rawls's statement and ordering of these principles have generated opposition on both egalitarian and libertarian grounds that not only mirrors but also underlies disputes that transpire in the political arena. As for the philosophical grounding, Anderson fails to see the practical implications of the disagreements between liberals and communitarians. Communitarians reject the contractarian basis for individual liberties; and while they do not necessarily seek to infringe upon those liberties in a wholesale manner, they do seek to justify them in the name of a common good. Yet they also may seek to restrict them in the name of a common good: the case of pornography is one where communitarians are far more likely than liberals to allow communities to adopt measures to eliminate what is widely thought to be deleterious to women in particular and society in general. Anderson fails to see both that what we call "academic" disputes are not confined to the academic community, and that what we call "political" disputes are not confined to the realm of politicians and bureaucrats.
51. See John Patrick Diggins, *The Promise of Pragmatism: Modernism and the Crisis of Knowledge and Authority* (Chicago: University of Chicago Press, 1994), 16, 434–36.
52. Ibid., 289.
53. Ibid., 435.
54. Ibid., 492.
55. Ibid., 428–34.
56. Ibid., 465 (italics added).
57. Ibid., 466.
58. Richard Rorty, "Postmodernist Bourgeois Liberalism," in *Hermeneutics and Praxis,* ed. Robert Hollinger (Notre Dame, Ind.: University of Notre Dame Press, 1985), 214–21.
59. Rorty, *Contingency, Irony, and Solidarity,* xv. Rorty acknowledges here that he borrows from Judith N. Shklar, *Ordinary Vices* (Cambridge: Harvard University Press, Belknap Press, 1984).

60. Rorty, *Contingency, Irony, and Solidarity,* 60–61.

61. Ibid., 63. Rorty has subsequently made clear that the prevention of suffering should include a welfare state to check the excesses of capitalism. See Richard Rorty, "For a More Banal Politics," *Harper's Magazine,* May 1992, 16–20.

62. Rorty, "Priority of Democracy," 258.

63. Ibid., 263.

64. Examples are Abraham Lincoln's suspension of the writ of habeas corpus in the Civil War and Franklin D. Roosevelt's internment of Japanese-Americans on the West Coast in World War II.

65. John Dewey, "Democracy and Educational Administration" (1937), in L11 (1987): 218. Most references to Dewey's writings in the notes are to the set of volumes published by Southern Illinois University Press in Carbondale and edited by Jo Ann Boydston. The volumes are divided into three series: *The Early Works, 1882–1898* (5 vols.), *The Middle Works, 1899–1924* (15 vols.), and *The Later Works, 1925–1953* (17 vols.). Initial references include, in order after Dewey's name, (1) the original work from which the quotation or reference was taken, (2) the original date of publication of that work in parentheses, (3) an abbreviation for the source from the Southern Illinois University set consisting of the series (E for *Early Works,* M for *Middle Works,* L for *Later Works*) and volume number (e.g., L11 for *Later Works,* vol. 11), (4) the date of publication of that volume in parentheses, and (5) the page number(s) from that volume following a colon.

66. Anderson, *Pragmatic Liberalism,* 164.

67. Ibid., 3–4.

68. Ibid., 3.

69. John Dewey, *The Public and Its Problems* (1927), in L2 (1984): 275. Hereafter I shall refer to this work parenthetically in the text as *PIP* followed by page number.

70. See the works of Friedrich Nietzsche.

71. Michael J. Sandel, "Dewey Rides Again," *New York Review of Books,* 9 May 1996, 37.

72. Ibid., 38. See also Michael J. Sandel, *Democracy's Discontent: America in Search of a Public Philosophy* (Cambridge: Harvard University Press, 1996).

73. Alfonso J. Damico, *Individuality and Community: The Social and Political Thought of John Dewey* (Gainesville: University Presses of Florida, 1978), 55n13.

74. Steven C. Rockefeller, *John Dewey: Religious Faith and Democratic Humanism* (New York: Columbia University Press, 1991), 73.

75. Ibid., 74.

76. John Dewey, *A Common Faith* (1934), in L9 (1986): 35. See also Corliss Lamont, "New Light on Dewey's *Common Faith,*" *Journal of Philosophy* 58

(1961): 21–28; Sidney Hook, *Pragmatism and the Tragic Sense of Life* (New York: Basic Books, 1974), 114.

77. Rockefeller, *John Dewey*, 73.

78. Robert B. Westbrook, *John Dewey and American Democracy* (Ithaca: Cornell University Press, 1991), xiv.

79. Ibid., 539–42.

80. Alan Ryan, *John Dewey and the High Tide of American Liberalism* (New York: Norton, 1995), 22, 21.

81. Ibid., 128.

82. Ibid., 192.

83. Ibid., 200.

84. Ibid., 230–31.

85. Ibid., 355.

86. Ibid., 228, 315.

87. Ibid., 219–20.

88. Ibid., 367.

89. Ibid., 368. "The bliss of solitude" is a phrase from Wordsworth.

90. Ibid., 367.

91. Ibid., 368.

92. Ibid., 367.

93. Ibid., 347. See Richard Hofstadter, *Anti-Intellectualism in American Life* (New York: Knopf, 1963).

94. David M. Steiner, *Rethinking Democratic Education: The Politics of Reform* (Baltimore: Johns Hopkins University Press, 1994), 127, 135, 175–79.

95. John Dewey and Arthur F. Bentley, *John Dewey and Arthur F. Bentley: A Philosophical Correspondence, 1932–1951,* ed. Sidney Ratner and Jules Altman (New Brunswick, N.J.: Rutgers University Press, 1964), 194.

96. James H. Nichols Jr., "Pragmatism and the U.S. Constitution," in *Confronting the Constitution,* ed. Allan Bloom (Washington, D.C.: AEI Press, 1990), 369.

97. Dewey and Bentley, *Philosophical Correspondence,* 242.

98. Sidney Hook, "Introduction," in L1 (1981): viii.

99. Richard J. Bernstein, "Philosophy in the Conversation of Mankind," *Review of Metaphysics* 33 (1980): 768.

100. For a thorough study of Dewey's transition from idealism to pragmatism, see Jennifer Welchman, *Dewey's Ethical Thought* (Ithaca: Cornell University Press, 1995). But I believe that Welchman overestimates, or at least misjudges, the possibility for ethics to take its bearings from modern science, even more than does Dewey.

101. John Dewey, "Nature in Experience" (1940), in L14 (1988): 150.

2

DEWEY'S REFORMULATION OF
LIBERALISM

Dewey's *The Public and Its Problems,* published in 1927, is in part the result of a disagreement with the preeminent journalist Walter Lippmann concerning the feasibility of a truly democratic society. Dewey's book is a response to two books written by Lippmann, *Public Opinion* (1922) and *The Phantom Public* (1925), in which Lippmann argued that the ability of a democratic people to govern itself faces insurmountable limits. The central problem, according to Lippmann, is the limited knowledge available to citizens both individually and collectively. Only social scientists have the resources needed to discover the truth about political questions, and a well-run political society is one where an economic and political elite make important decisions on the basis of facts provided by social scientists. All that citizens can do is to "support the Ins when things are going well; to support the Outs when they seem to be going badly."[1]

Dewey is not persuaded of that conclusion. Reviewing *Public Opinion,* he admits that "there is nothing about which men are more confused than their interests"; but he concludes, "The enlightenment of public opinion still seems to me to have priority over the enlightenment of officials and directors."[2] In a review of *The Phantom Public,* he says that Lippmann's plan to have decisions made with limited public involvement would itself not work without "the further organization of society."[3] In *The Public and Its Problems* he elaborates on that remark. He agrees with Lippmann that the American citizenry is not in good position at the time to make self-governing judgments. But he disagrees with Lippmann's view that the limitations cannot be overcome.

In this chapter I explore the possibilities of Dewey's political thought as an alternative to liberal individualism. I begin with the question of public and private; but Dewey's answer to that question is not so detailed as we might like. The notion of community is central to his political thought, and I examine the ability of Deweyan liberalism to provide a sense of community. I then consider the ability of Deweyan liberalism to avoid certain ills to which liberal politics are susceptible, and its ability to avoid one of the ills that liberal democracy was designed to avoid: the tyranny of the majority. I draw on a number of Dewey's works, including some that do not fall strictly within the field of political theory.

DEWEY'S NOTION OF THE PUBLIC

The Public and Its Problems is Dewey's most thorough attempt to return to first political principles and his fullest treatment of political theory. He begins it by remarking on the importance of discerning what the state is, rather than what it should be; he finds "the key to the nature and office of the state" in the distinction between private and public (*PIP*, 245). Some actions have consequences that affect only "the persons directly engaged in a transaction," while the consequences of other actions "affect others beyond those immediately concerned" (*PIP*, 243–44). The former sort of action is properly considered private; the latter, public.

Those who are indirectly affected by the actions of others need someone to look after their interests. Dewey assumes that they will be too numerous to make regulatory decisions completely by themselves. Representatives and other public officials constitute the government; but they do not by themselves form the state, for the state includes the public as well as the government. Dewey defines the state as "the organization of the public effected through officials for the protection of the interests shared by its members" (*PIP*, 256).

How far does the state extend? Dewey claims that "the line between private and public is to be drawn on the basis of the extent and scope of the consequences of acts which are so important as to need control, whether by inhibition or by promotion" (*PIP*, 245). He insists that the limits of the state cannot be specified in advance; rather they must be determined experimentally. As further guidance he adds that public actions can be known by "the far-reaching character of consequences, whether in space or time; their settled, uniform and recurrent nature, and their irreparableness" (*PIP*, 275). Yet Dewey refuses to call any particular association private. In principle the state may "fix conditions under which *any* form of association operates" (*PIP*, 280).

Dewey's lack of a fixed attachment to any set of democratic institutions shows his experimentalism. "There is no sanctity in universal suffrage, frequent elections, majority rule, congressional and cabinet government" (*PIP*, 326). They are to be modified to suit the needs of the state to perform its regulatory function. The key precondition for the attainment of this end is awareness on the part of the members of the public that they constitute a public—an awareness that they have an interest in common with one another. This key precondition is also the central problem; for, Dewey writes, the "democratic public is still largely inchoate and unorganized" (*PIP*, 303). The large scale of modern society has extended the area over which consequences of actions have effect, and in an impersonal way, so that a public does not know that it exists. It is indeed more accurate to say "a public" than "the public," for, according to Dewey, a distinctive body of citizens is formed every time a transaction has indirect consequences. In modern times, Dewey says, there are "too many publics and too much of public concern for our existing resources to cope with" (*PIP*, 314).

Thus the central political problem for Dewey is to facilitate the self-identification of publics. Accomplishing this goal requires "improvement of the methods and conditions of debate, discussion and persuasion," which in turn depends upon "freeing and perfecting the processes of inquiry and of dissemination of their conclusions" (*PIP*, 365). On the one hand, Dewey recognizes that much of this inquiry will be performed by experts, not by the majority of people; on the other hand, he concludes *The Public and Its Problems* by stressing the importance of local communities, through which the results of inquiry must work in the formation of public opinion. Public opinion must be prepared to judge the work of experts in terms of the public interest or interests.

The purpose of that inquiry—the purpose of the state itself—is not aggrandizement of the state, but promotion of the peaceful and fruitful functioning of the associations that make up local communities.[4] "When a state is a good state, when the officers of the public genuinely serve the public interests, this reflex effect [i.e., of the state on private associations] is of great importance. It renders the desirable associations solider and more coherent; indirectly it clarifies their aims and purges their activities. . . . In performing these services, it gives the individual members of valued associations greater liberty and security" (*PIP,* 279–80). In contrast to the individualistic tradition, Dewey defines liberty as "that secure release and fulfillment of personal potentialities which take place only in rich and manifold association with others" and equality as "the unhampered share which each individual member of the community has in the consequences of associated action" (*PIP,* 329).

If the distinction between private and public is the key to understanding the state, Dewey says relatively little about that distinction. He observes that the terms "individual" and "social" are not correspondingly equivalent to "private" and "public," because private acts may have social consequences and yet not be deemed public (*PIP,* 244). For example, a philanthropist's donations may have widespread effects, but those donations are not publicly required. We could hope for more examples than the few Dewey gives, however.

Why does Dewey not say more to delineate public and private? First, his experimental approach to the state means that not much more can be said. That approach insists on taking into account the particulars of a situation before making a decision; although the giving of examples provides particulars more than theorizing does, even examples are something of an abstraction. There is no substitute for examining all of the facts prior to a decision.

Second, Dewey does not want us to consider the two spheres of public and private as inherently separate, as we might tend to do. The danger would be that we would forget the interdependence of the two. As we have seen, for Dewey public officials cannot do their jobs well unless they keep in mind the associations that often function privately. As we shall see, conversely, for Dewey success in the private sphere requires involvement in the public life. He is not willing to say that any particular social group will be private per se because actions of any group may be sufficiently "far-reaching" and important to warrant public response or regulation.

THE PUBLIC AS ALTERNATIVE TO CIVIL SOCIETY

It is the absence of a firm distinction between public and private that, among other things, Dewey believes separates his liberalism from previous liberalisms. An account of liberty as "release and fulfillment of personal potentialities" is not mere freedom from restraint; it is freedom to do something. He goes further. His view of the origin of the state is directly opposed to the tradition of liberal individualism and the social contract. The state does not arise "by direct conscious intent" (*PIP,* 259). He continues, "The idea of a natural individual in his isolation possessed of full-fledged wants, of energies to be expended according to his own volition, and of a ready-made faculty of foresight and prudent calculation is as much a fiction in psychology as the doctrine of the individual in possession of antecedent political rights is one in politics" (*PIP,* 299).

Dewey's notion of a public or publics has the role in his thought that civil or political society has in earlier liberal thought, especially that of Locke. For Locke the unanimous act of individuals leaving the state of nature establishes a civil society; the first and only independent act of that civil society is to decide by majority rule where to place the legislative power, which Locke describes—following Hobbes—as "*the Soul that gives Form, Life, and Unity* to the Commonwealth."[5] For Dewey, in contrast to both Hobbes and Locke, it is at least one "public" that is created—theoretically—before the government and hence the state, and the state "comes into existence" in order to regulate the indirect consequences of actions (*PIP,* 244). "Society" as a unity is not meaningful for Dewey; he says that "there is no one *thing* which may be called society, except" the "indefinite overlapping" of private associations (*PIP,* 279).

Hobbes and Locke, along with other social contract thinkers, agree on the basic point that civil society is an association of independent human beings. The same is true even for Hegel, who makes use of the notion of civil society despite rejecting the idea of the social contract.[6] Hegel defines civil society as "an association of members as self-subsistent individuals in a universality"; the "concrete person" (i.e., not the abstract subject) is "one principle of civil society."[7] As Pierre Hassner has noted, civil society for Hegel represents a "moment of separation and difference."[8]

For Dewey, the notion of the public represents a moment not of "separation and difference," but of unity and similarity. The creation of a public marks a coming together on the part of a group of individuals who were previously separate (functionally, not metaphysically, speaking). It also signifies the recognition of a commonality by those people, who until then might have seen themselves as having only the barest minimum of shared purposes.

Yet Locke's civil society and Dewey's public both represent unity and similarity. How then does Dewey's public differ from the traditional liberal notion of civil society? One main difference lies in the degree of unity available. Civil society for Locke can never be more than a qualified solidarity: the qualification resides in the right that each individual retains to act for his self-preservation. The individual surrenders the power to do what he thinks fit for his self-preservation only "so far forth" as his preservation permits, because people "will always have a right to preserve what they have not a Power to part with."[9] It is simply not in accordance with human nature for harmony among the members of a civil society to be guaranteed. The individual is properly concerned primarily with himself and his own preservation; but as Locke says, "the preservation of the Society" is its "first and fundamental natural Law," the rule by which it must govern itself.[10]

But what individual would find his preservation in competition with the preservation of society? We must not exaggerate the conflict between individual and community for Locke. For there seem to be only three possibilities here: an individual who threatens the preservation of society—in other words, a violent criminal—would find himself in such a conflict with society; or an innocent individual might be threatened by a misguided community; or an individual, such as a soldier, might be asked to give his life for his country. Yet we must not inaccurately minimize the division between individual and society either: the passion for self-preservation, which Locke calls our "imperious Passion," is one way or another always with us.[11] We are therefore in one way or another always reminded of the impossibility of complete unity. Peter Laslett claims that Locke views the "law of *universal* preservation as the fundamental natural law."[12] But Laslett neglects here that, according to Locke, the duty to the "Preservation of all Mankind" takes second for each individual to the duty "to preserve himself."[13] This duty, or natural law, or natural right, of each person is not to be forgotten in politics by any prudent citizen—be that citizen an officeholder or not. Nevertheless, Laslett is certainly correct to suggest that the "law of universal preservation" becomes the purpose of political association, generally viewed: as Locke puts it, "the mutual *Preservation* of their [i.e., persons'] Lives, Liberties and Estates, which I call by the general Name, *Property*."[14]

By contrast, Dewey holds out the hope of complete unity or integration between individual and society. Dewey does not expect a problem-free society, one in which individuals never encounter difficulties or find themselves at odds with one another or with society. In fact he expects new problems to arise as old ones are solved. But he does envision and hope for an absence of hostility among people, an absence of a state of affairs in which people see no possibility of harmonization of their goals and thus the need to contest one another. So little is human nature fixed in its needs or the manifestations of those needs according to Dewey that, while he is willing to grant a general, natural need for combat, he does not admit that combat must take the form of individuals' opposing one another.[15] (I shall examine Dewey's conception of human nature further in chapter 3.)

It is characteristic of Dewey's thought that he refuses to consider the individual except in relation to society, and (usually) society except in terms of the individuals who constitute it. As early as 1897, while he was still in his neo-Hegelian phase, Dewey expressed the purpose of the education of an individual entirely in terms of socialization, "participation in social life." "Society is a society of individuals and the individual is always a social individual. He has no existence by himself. He lives in, for, and by society, just as society has no existence excepting in and through the individuals who constitute it." The standard of moral worth is not the individual but "the larger life" of the individual in society.[16] In 1930 he writes, "Assured and integrated individuality is the product of definite social relationships and publicly acknowledged functions."[17] At the beginning of the final chapter of *The Public and Its Problems,* Dewey criticizes early modern liberalism for its ahistorical, asocial individualism by claiming that it is not even possible to define the term "individual" without reference to what he considers the necessary link between the individual and the social—a link that he expresses in such works as *Individualism, Old and New.* It is not possible to define an individual strictly in terms of separateness; points of contiguity with others must also be recognized.[18]

I do not mean to imply that there was not a change of emphasis in his views over time. We may contrast the article of 1897, where the standard of moral worth is said to be the society, with an article of 1939, in which Dewey writes, "I should now wish to emphasize more than I formerly did that individuals are the finally decisive factors of the nature and movement of associated life." He admits that political events of the previous few years had caused this change in emphasis and led him to conclude that "individuals who prize their own liberties and who prize the liberties of other individuals, individuals who are democratic in thought and action, are the sole final warrant for the existence and endurance of democratic institutions."[19] Does this mark a change in emphasis merely, or a more fundamental change of position? I would say the former: even in 1939 Dewey never claims that we can define the individual apart from the larger society.

Throughout his career Dewey insists, particularly in his works on education, that there is no conflict between the good of a fully developed individual and the good of society. The child naturally wants "to serve" his fellows in society, and educators must understand that the "law" in intellectual and spiritual affairs is "co-operation and participation."[20] "What one is as a person is what one is as associated with others, in a free give and take of intercourse." That the activities of life are bound up with emotions appears to indicate that there is no separate inner world for an individual apart from his relations with others.[21]

Dewey's opposition to traditional liberal individualism is not a rejection of liberalism per se. Indeed Dewey remains a liberal in three major respects. First, he advocates government by deliberate decision making. Decisions about the regulation of indirect consequences of actions in the public interest are to be made either by citizens themselves or by their representatives; for Dewey participatory democracy does not mean the illegitimacy of representative democracy. Particular representative institutions have nothing venerable about them, but Dewey clearly believes in the need for some sort of institution in which officers of the citizenry will gather to make judgments in the public interest (*PIP*, 283, 287).

Second, Dewey favors limited government. Although his experimentalism will not allow a specification of any definite limits to the scope of government, he teaches that the purpose of government is to facilitate and enhance the activities of associations, not to envelop them in a larger entity called the state (*PIP*, 279–81). The state is "a distinctive and secondary form of association, having a specifiable work to do and specified organs of operation" (*PIP*, 279). He writes that "only the voluntary initiative and voluntary cooperation of individuals can produce social institutions that will protect the liberties necessary for achieving development of genuine individuality."[22]

Third, Dewey wants to preserve a wide range of individual rights. In the 1930s he was accused of encouraging a dangerous collectivism; and he did not always stress the need for individual rights, as the aforementioned article of 1939 makes clear in concession. Dewey consistently criticizes the liberal individualism of the early modern period for its ahistoricism, but he concurs with the individual rights of the Declaration of Independence, although he prefers the adjective "moral" to "natural" when speaking of rights.[23]

The heart of Dewey's political project is to retain the essential features of liberalism while removing them from their individualistic base. This means recasting our understanding of the place of individual rights in liberalism. Locke begins with individual freedom and derives the qualified unity of civil society from that freedom; Dewey wants to respect individual rights but also to understand them in a social context of complete unity or integration (again, in the sense of a possible absence of hostility, not in the sense of a total absence of problems). For example, he credits Oliver Wendell Holmes and Louis D. Brandeis "not only for their sturdy defense of civil liberties but even more for the fact that they based their defense on the indispensable value of free inquiry and free discussion to the normal development of public welfare, not upon anything inherent in the individual as such."[24] This recasting is the purpose of *Liberalism and Social Action,* where he argues that the securing of the individuality and freedom of inquiry that lie at the heart of liberalism requires the following: (1) an understanding of the "historic relativity" of ideas, according to which liberty depends on the social conditions existing at a given time; (2) "[o]rganized social planning" so that all citizens can have a sufficient material basis for their development; (3) a reordering of priorities, made possible by the previous development, in which material concerns are subordinated to "cultural values"; and (4) reform of political institutions that will take into account "occupational groups and the organized knowledge and purposes that are involved in the existence of such groups" so that we shall not see the public interest as defined by "a summation of individuals quantitatively."[25]

Lockean politics are dominated by the worst-case scenario: the situation in which preservation is in jeopardy. Politics thus aim at the prevention of the worst possible outcome instead of the best outcome conceivable to human beings; or rather, prevention of the worst becomes the best to which human beings aspire in political association. Deweyan politics, on the other hand, are not dominated to any significant extent by the worst-case scenario. It is thus possible to aim higher, at the flourishing of individuality within society—and, what Dewey sees as higher, at the full integration of all individuals within society. That integration is available through the peaceful, everyday solving of conflicts as they arise. By contrast, for Hegel it takes the extreme case—war—to achieve a full unity of citizens, because only in war is the superiority of state to civil society manifest.[26] Yet while we may say that Dewey aims higher than Locke, he is not so ambitious as Marx, who anticipates the supplanting of civil society upon a recognition of the human species as a universal fellowship.[27]

What more precisely do I mean by "aiming higher"? Let me try to make this distinction between Locke and Dewey more specific. Criticisms of the aims of liberal individualist politics have a long history, even predating liberal individualism itself.[28] More recently those criticisms have been made in a noteworthy manner by Rousseau, among others. Rousseau's attack on Lockean politics boils down to two related arguments. First, in a state based on the self-preservation of the individual, and even universal preservation more generally, each person will see his own welfare as at least potentially opposed to the welfare of others and will pursue his own at the expense of others'. Because Lockean political association exists to preserve possessions, and in particular because Locke introduces money into the state of nature, the result will be a society featuring the rich few and the poor many. The laws will favor the former at the expense of the latter, and in effect money will become the standard of human dignity. Second, and even apart from economic considerations, the fact that society is based on the calculation of each person's private advantage destroys the foundation of trust among citizens, producing instead "mutual hate." Good citizens cannot come to exist in such conditions; hence neither can happiness, without which preservation is useless.[29]

THE WORKINGS OF AN ACTIVE PUBLIC

How would an understanding of politics based on Dewey's notion of the public attempt to escape those charges? What hope might it offer political theorists seeking to avoid those alleged problems of liberal society? First we must note that a public is not something that a person enters because of a prior individual freedom, as is the case with Locke's civil society. For Locke, it is the individual's right and duty of self-preservation that lead him to leave the "Inconveniences of the State of Nature, which must certainly be Great," and enter a society under the protection of government.[30] For Dewey, it is also the noticing of actions with unfavorable consequences that leads to the taking of collective action. But a public is not something that people enter from a prior standpoint of a self-sufficient individuality. Because it is not, the hope exists that, insofar as the origin of the public helps to determine its workings, those workings will not be dominated by each individual's thought that he has something to protect at the expense of everyone and everything else.

Nor is the motivation of individuals the only difference. Dewey's public is a grouping of human beings in the formation of which the rights of individuals are not a focus. To be sure, Dewey's analysis of the creation of a public presupposes certain individual rights. It is impossible to see how a public can discern the indirect consequences of previously private transactions, select officials to represent them, or ensure that those officials serve their interest unless individuals enjoy the liberties of speech, press, and association. If Dewey had a notion of group rights that he wished to substitute for individual rights at this point in his argument, he surely would have mentioned it here. But he seems to imply that during the formation and existence of a public, the focus should remain on the commonalities of those similarly affected by the transaction; the fact that all members of a public enjoy certain rights is merely a means to recognizing those commonalities and acting on them.[31] Individual rights do not ground or control Dewey's political theory. Again, because the process of forming a public does not involve an emphasis on individual rights, the unity of a public should be easier to maintain.

Because of the absence of a focus on individual rights, there is at least a possibility that each person may be led to see his own welfare in terms of the welfare of others. In the formation of a public, a person who sees himself affected by the transactions of others cannot help seeing that other people are likewise affected. He sees the solution to his problem as inextricably connected to a solution to the same problem that affects those other people. Moreover, a solution to his problem requires that he cooperate with others. Now it is true that the formation of a public also involves a recognition of an opposition of interests, in the many cases where the transactions of previously private individuals adversely affect others.[32] But, as Dewey sees it, that formation also marks the beginning of an attempt to resolve that opposition peacefully. Dewey seeks to preserve the mutual trust that Rousseau sees as absent from liberal politics by maintaining a sense that all citizens are engaged in a common enterprise, so that the possibility exists for a full integration of every individual within society. We shall see shortly in more detail how he hopes to maintain that sense.

First it is worth noting that the protection of property is not central to the formation of a public for Dewey, as is the case with Locke's civil society. In fact it is the sanctity of the right to private property that Dewey repeatedly blames for the difficulty that the members of a potential public have in recognizing their common interest. That sanctity, he writes in 1918, echoing Rousseau, has led to an American society in which too many people lack basic subsistence. As a remedy Dewey goes so far as to propose a new individual right: "The first great demand of a better social order, . . . is the guarantee of the right, to every individual who is capable of it, to work—not the mere legal right, but a right which is enforceable."[33]

But Dewey believes that the provision of the right to work and an adequate standard of living would not be sufficient to enable the members of a public to be in position to recognize the indirect consequences of actions affecting them. What is also required is industrial democracy, a condition in which workers in all occupations have fundamental control over the social and economic circumstances of their lives. Dewey has been accused, and justifiably so, of a lack of specificity concerning the meaning of democratic citizenship.[34] But he does make clear that state socialism is incompatible with a democratic citizenship that permits self-identification of a public.[35] Otherwise, it is true, Dewey does not offer much detail on the desirable end beyond calling for "a federation of self-governing industries."[36] (In the 1930s, however, he is more specific on the means, proposing large-scale public works and the socialization of basic resources and utilities.)[37]

Dewey does not appear to be entirely consistent, or at least clear, on the degree of political activity that he expects from the citizens of a state. On the one hand, Dewey makes it seem that a public will act ultimately through its elected officials: "the primary problem of the public," he says, is "to achieve such recognition of itself as will give it weight in the selection of official representatives and in the definition of their responsibilities and rights" (*PIP,* 283). Whether "primary" in this context means first or leading is unclear. Only five years after publication of *The Public and Its Problems* he coauthored a second edition of a widely used textbook, *Ethics,* with James H. Tufts in which he seems to concede some truth to the often-made criticism of participatory democracy that "the number [of people] capable of independent and original thinking" is necessarily small:

> Admitting the most extreme statement that can be rendered plausible concerning the innate intellectual inferiority of the mass, the alleged inferiority concerns their ability to originate and create, not to take in and to follow. They may be, as Plato said, predestined to live on the level of opinion rather than of understanding, but also, as he pointed out, they may absorb and be guided by right opinion.[38]

If this is all a public is capable of, then what more can be hoped for than that people will be discerning enough to judge the rhetoric of their leaders' competing speeches and not eventually become so cynical about the entire political process that they allow elites to govern unchecked?[39]

Yet it is clear that Dewey expects a public to do more than merely judge rhetoric in order to ascertain true opinion. First, leaders cannot be counted on to organize a public. It is true that for Dewey the creation of a public does not have to lead to the establishment of a new state or even a significant modification of the structure of the old one. A public may rely on already elected leaders to accomplish the task of securing its interest. But it cannot expect those elected leaders to do the work of making its members aware of their common interest—particularly when a conflicting interest, which those leaders may have been selected to represent, may be involved.

This leads to another difficulty: in practice no one will be a member of only one public. Each person will be affected by the indirect consequences of many different transactions. Thus not only the officials but the citizens also will have conflicting public interests. In the case of each different transaction affecting him, a person will need to be able to do the following things: participate in the defining of that particular public interest and hence the organization of the public; select officials to represent that interest; and help to guarantee that those officials serve that interest. Moreover, each person will need to be able to relate his conflicting public interests to one another in order to judge how those interests may best be served. It is in keeping with Dewey's philosophy on the whole that he does not speak of an overall objective "public interest," an Archimedean point from which citizens might hope to assess the relative merits of their conflicting interests.

It is very likely that no two citizens will have the exact same collection of public interests; no two citizens will belong to the very same set of publics. Moreover, each citizen will have a unique understanding of each of his public interests because he sees it in relation to others. And with those two facts a more fundamental problem in Dewey's political theory arises: how could a citizen attempting to judge in a Deweyan manner not tend to see himself as ultimately alone in the political world? How could he not slip into an individualistic way of thinking that would be at least potentially disuniting for politics?

Dewey's best answer to those questions appears to be human psychology, as a necessary condition, and education, as a necessary and sufficient condition. Dewey's psychological theory revolves around an understanding of "habit" as something other than the routine conduct of an individual. Habit means "human activity which is influenced by prior activity and in that sense acquired"; "an acquired predisposition to *ways* or modes of response, not to particular acts except as, under special conditions, these express a way of behaving." Because they are acquired, they are always social. "It is not an ethical 'ought' that conduct *should* be social. It *is* social, whether bad or good."[40] Human psychology also involves "impulses," the natural tendencies of individual human beings. But, as I have noted, those natural tendencies do not take a specific direction on their own; the influence of habits comes into play in shaping impulses and causing them to have a particular manifestation. Education involves the shaping of impulses through the formation of habits.

And for Dewey education well conducted is education with a focus on the scientific method, a method that involves cooperation and thus is friendly to democracy. "It is of the nature of science not so much to tolerate as to welcome diversity of opinion, while it insists that inquiry brings the evidence of observed facts to bear to effect a consensus of conclusions. . . . [F]reedom of inquiry, toleration of diverse views, freedom of communication, the distribution of what is found out to every individual as the ultimate intellectual consumer, are involved in the democratic as in the scientific method."[41] Dewey's educational theory emphasizes nothing more than scientific method as "the method of intelligence."

Dewey's notion of scientific method is that of a reflective process consisting of several steps: (a) "perplexity"; (b) "a conjectural anticipation"; (c) "a careful survey" of all considerations; (d) "elaboration of the tentative hypothesis to make it more precise and more consistent"; (e) acting upon the hypothesis in order to test it (*DE*, 157). These steps are guidelines, not rigid rules to be followed in every scientific inquiry. The exact method of one inquirer will vary from that of another "as his original instinctive capacities vary, as his past experiences and his preferences vary" (*DE*, 180). Trained in this method from a young age, people will see that their future possibilities depend on the way in which others conduct their lives; hence they will willingly grant to others the most extensive liberties possible. Harmony of the individual with society is impossible without the construction of democratic publics modeled on a scientific community; with such education, though, Dewey seems to think that harmonious integration is possible.

I asked how Dewey could prevent individualistic thinking from perverting democratic politics. As we have seen, his answer turns to psychology and education. A human being *cannot* see himself as an isolated individual—he is simply not constituted that way, it seems there is no human "self" apart from the sum of habits that inform an individual's character—and, to the extent to which he is well educated, his thinking and conduct will take a socially beneficial direction. How good is that answer?

First we may ask, how solid is the kinship between science and democracy? Does scientific method at its highest exemplify a social group in which intelligence is socialized? On the one hand, comparison to science may lift up democratic practice by giving it a goal to strive for—the truth or reasonable desire—instead of the desire of the moment. On the other hand, science does not always operate through democratic means. In fact some would say that many of the greatest scientific achievements have come when at least one of the five steps mentioned by Dewey has been violated, or when diverse views have not been fully tolerated, or when one person has worked alone. Moreover, as Dewey is well aware, science does not always operate for democratic ends (*FC*, 156). Thus, in criticism of Marxism for its claim to be scientific despite its unscientific ways, he says that we may learn of "the *potential* alliance between scientific and democratic method and the need of consummating this potentiality in the techniques of legislation and administration" (*FC*, 135; italics added). Let those points be widely understood and training in scientific method may yield a preference for non-democratic politics.

Second, we may ask whether Dewey's psychology solves the problem we have noted. How could a citizen attempting to judge in a Deweyan manner not tend to see himself as ultimately alone in the political world? It is not enough for Dewey to say that human beings are inherently social creatures, even including the possibility of hostility toward society. The point made by the problem is precisely that the educative influence of Dewey's political theory, with its invitation for us to consider the practical workings of publics, will be at least as strong as, if not stronger than, the influence of his psychological and educational theory. Acquired habits of thought of a common enterprise or a harmony among the interests of individuals will likely be overpowered by the daily thought of uniqueness of combination of interests and uniqueness of particular interests. It appears that, despite its attempt to reject the individualism of traditional liberal thought and politics, Dewey's liberalism cannot avoid what we (and readers of Dewey have often made this criticism) might call human separateness—that is, the character of what separates one human being from another.

Upon further examination of Dewey's conception of individuality, however, I cannot maintain that conclusion.[42] For example, he writes, "Individuality itself is originally a potentiality and is realized only in interaction with surrounding conditions. In this process of intercourse, native capacities, which contain an element of uniqueness, are transformed and become a self."[43] With this "element of uniqueness" we see that Dewey acknowledges a character that distinguishes one human being from another. It is not that human nature is individual, rather "that human nature, like other forms of life, tends to differentiation, and this moves in the direction of the distinctively individual, and that it also tends toward combination, association" (*FC*, 77–78). Individuality lasts over time; it is not dissolved in a totality. Yet a person's individuality cannot always clearly be seen at any one moment. Indeed it can be found only over time: individuality "is found only in life-history, in its continuing growth; it is, so to say, a career and not just a fact discoverable at a particular cross section of life."[44]

Whether or not his account is correct, Dewey does attempt to explain what separates one human being from another. To say that he runs up against human separateness here would be to make a metaphysical claim for existential discontinuity that I do not want to make, because I do not know that it would be justified. What I do find unjustified in Dewey is his conviction concerning a lack of ultimate tension among the goods of different people. If a tension does exist, individualistic thinking may preclude the political outcomes that he desires. The "Great Community" that Dewey envisions may not live up to his expectations.

DEWEY AND THE LIBERAL VS. COMMUNITARIAN DEBATE

More precisely, what can a study of Dewey teach us about the kind of community possible in a liberal society? Two of the leading members of the current communitarian school are Alasdair MacIntyre and Michael Sandel. MacIntyre's critique of the philosophical foundations of liberalism is an attack on the Enlightenment claim that all moral, social, and political problems are solvable through reason independent of any particular political tradition. Hence, he says, we children of the Enlightenment expect of our politics that it can take us as naturally isolated individuals, deny us any recourse to a shared conception of the good life, and make us live harmoniously together. The result is the divisiveness of unending argument on fundamental moral questions. A solution to this conflict will require new political institutions. "What matters at this stage is the construction of local forms of community within which civility and the intellectual and moral life can be sustained through the new dark ages which are already upon us."[45]

Sandel emphasizes the need to reconceptualize liberal institutions. In order to achieve the priority of justice desired by liberals such as John Rawls and Robert Nozick, liberals must hold an incredible metaphysical view about the self: that personal identity exists completely separate from relations, attachments, or goals. Sandel asserts instead that we are "subjects constituted in part by our central aspirations and attachments."[46]

Sandel's description of Dewey as a "communitarian liberal" appears to be apt. We have seen that Dewey wants to retain the essential features of liberalism while he removes it from its individualist base. As for community, Dewey says, "The Great Society created by steam and electricity may be a society, but it is no community" (*PIP*, 296). "Extensive, enduring, intricate and serious indirect consequences of the conjoint activity of a comparatively few persons traverse the globe. . . . The need is that the non-political [especially economic] forces organize themselves to transform existing political structures: that the divided and troubled publics integrate" (*PIP*, 315). The key precondition for the organization of such a "Great Community" is improved communication among people and peoples (*PIP*, 324). The development of strong local communities, which he stresses at the end of *The Public and Its Problems,* is a key step toward the creation of the "Great Community."

Dewey's notion of plural publics is essential for understanding the character of his communitarianism. Every public whose members recognize themselves as forming a public has engaged in communication such that we might call it a community; Dewey's ideal of the national, "Great Community" reveals his belief that geographic proximity is not an essential characteristic of community. In a true democracy, a public will be a community of interests within the "Great Community." Those interests may at times conflict with one another; but as a community its members will be committed to resolving them through cooperative inquiry.

Here, then, is Dewey's contribution to the formulation of communitarianism: his belief that many "publics" can exist within one large community. One scholar, Avigail Eisenberg, claims that Dewey's pluralism of publics separates him from communitarianism.[47] But I think that it is more accurate to say that Dewey's formulation of pluralism is his contribution to communitarianism, so loosely is the term "communitarian" used in academic discourse. At least one theorist often associated with communitarianism, Michael Walzer, actively defends pluralism, if by "pluralism" we mean the existence of diverse, mainly autonomous social groups within a common civil society.[48] Moreover, Sandel does not advocate for his country the strict subservience of individual rights to a national, common good.[49] Sandel's recognition of the need for pluralism is perhaps rooted in his claim that we are constituted in part by our attachments and purposes: We may infer that in part we are *not* constituted by our attachments and purposes, that the notion of the "unencumbered self" that he finds in Rawls is not entirely inaccurate. Thus it is impossible that the citizens of a nation, or even of a local community, could ever have their identity completely defined by a single, common good, and it is at best pointless to try to enforce a single conception. To say the least, then, not all communitarians are antipluralist.

When Dewey says that the state must be able to regulate the conditions under which any form of association operates, some critics have taken him to be hostile to pluralism.[50] But the matter is not so simple. We may first ask two questions in order to gauge Dewey's pluralism: Does Dewey institute clear limits to the control of the state over associations? Does Dewey provide sufficient theoretical basis for the existence of groups? As for the first question, we have seen that Dewey will not allow specification of any definite limits to the scope of governmental control; limits must be determined experimentally. We might then conclude that Dewey's political theory is less successful than traditional liberalism, as defined by Locke. As for the second question, Dewey's theory of publics provides greater specificity than does Locke's liberalism, and greater than Sandel's communitarianism.

AVOIDING THE TYRANNY OF PUBLIC OPINION

Communitarianism is often associated with majoritarianism, or even identified with it. Majoritarianism is sometimes associated with the phrase "tyranny of the majority," coined by Tocqueville. As we examine the potential of Dewey's notion of the public or publics to serve as an alternative to the traditional notion of civil society, we must take stock of its ability not only to avoid the ills to which liberal politics are susceptible, but also to escape the ills that liberal democracy was designed to avoid. While one of those ills has been the tyrannical ruler or rulers, another threat, often more subtle than tyrannical government, is the tyranny of the majority. In examining the ability of Deweyan liberalism to avoid the latter condition, we are not subjecting his thought to a concern that was foreign to him. Indeed it was his concern: as we have seen, Dewey does not want the state to swallow up all private associations (*PIP,* 279–80). Can the more active publics that he desires keep from transforming themselves into majority tyranny?

We might initially conclude that a state with more active publics would not be dangerous. First, there is the simple fact of numerous publics within one state, rather than one large civil society. Second, it follows that two individuals who have the same interest on one matter, and thus are part of one public, will likely oppose each other on another matter, and thus not both be part of that public. Thus the majority on any question is likely to consist of a different public or collection of publics that have negotiated to reach a mutually acceptable solution. Third, the possibility exists that different publics will each have their own political representation, perhaps even with some sort of veto power in the legislative process, thus reducing the ability of a majority to act decisively.

But, particularly because Dewey teaches that the only limits to the scope of public authority cannot be determined in advance and must be set experimentally, we cannot dispense with the potential problem of majority tyranny so quickly. We must consider in more detail the dangers that can follow from majority tyranny and see what remedies Dewey's thought offers to them.

Those dangers received an important formulation in the work of Tocqueville. Tocqueville points to four main threats, and it is reasonable to suggest that American politics and society have suffered from all four, to an extent, at some point in the past or do suffer today. Thus I use Tocqueville's thought here to compare and contrast with Dewey's.

In *Democracy in America,* Tocqueville begins his analysis of the subject by noting, "The moral authority of the majority is partly based on the notion that there is more enlightenment and wisdom in a numerous assembly than in a single man, and the number of the legislators is more important than how they are chosen," and it is partly based on the view that "the interest of the greatest number should be preferred to that of those who are fewer." From there he proceeds to identify four dangerous effects to be expected from "the absolute sovereignty of the will of the majority."[51]

The first of these is "the legislative and administrative instability" that is already "natural to democracies" and increases along with the power of the majority. The cause of this instability is that "it is in the nature of democracies to bring new men to power." The premise implied in this cause is that public opinion tends to be changeable. Thus when the American people gave their "sovereign power" to a legislative body, they gave it the authority to "carry out anything it desires quickly and irresistibly." The instability is heightened by the American practice of frequent elections. As for administration, since "the majority is the only power whom it is important to please, all its projects are taken up with great ardor; but as soon as its attention is turned elsewhere, all these efforts cease." The American system provides for "zeal and energy" in administration. But, as he suggests in the example of the "pious people" who tried to promote the rehabilitation of criminals by building new prisons and yet allowed the old ones to deteriorate, zeal and energy are not sufficient to enable a people to strike the right chord between excessive gentleness and excessive barbarism.[52]

Omnipotence of the majority also serves to promote "arbitrary power" among office holders. Tocqueville contrasts arbitrary power, which is the use of authority undetermined by law, with tyranny, which is the use of power for the sake of the rulers instead of the ruled. Popular sovereignty opposes tyranny; but because the majority, "equally controlling both rulers and ruled, regards public functionaries as its passive agents," it is "glad to leave them the trouble of carrying out its plans. It therefore does not enter by anticipation into the details of their duties and hardly takes the trouble to define their rights." So confident is a majority of its ultimate control that not only does the law (presumably including the Constitution) allow wide latitude to public officials in their actions, it also allows those officials to go "beyond that"—Tocqueville presumably means against the law—as long as it is for the public good. "Thus habits form in freedom that may one day become fatal to that freedom."[53]

A third aspect of majority tyranny—and the one most revealing for Tocqueville because it most clearly separated America from the Europe of his day—is the power of the majority over thought. Freedom of thought and speech, which one would think to be more secure and effective in a democracy than in another form of government, is actually less so, at least in America: "while the majority is in doubt, one talks; but when it has irrevocably pronounced, everyone is silent, and friends and enemies alike seem to make for its bandwagon." The cause of this is the aforementioned moral authority vested in a majority in a democracy, which, combined with its visible power, produces a tyranny that "leaves the body alone" but "goes straight for the soul" in an irresistible way. Tocqueville concludes famously, "I know no country in which, speaking generally, there is less independence of mind and true freedom of discussion than in America"; and he makes the even stronger claim that "there is no freedom of the spirit in America." This intellectual homogeneity prevents indecent thoughts and books from being published. But it also prepares the way for a popular acceptance of "despotism."⁵⁴

Tocqueville relates that despotism and a fourth and final effect of tyranny of the majority to the American "national character." He contrasts the time of the American founding, when the leaders of the Revolution "had a greatness all their own," with his day, which he says is characterized by a "rareness . . . of outstanding men on the political scene" and an absence of patriotism among leaders. The essence of the problem is that the majority demands that a citizen either bow before it or "in a sense renounce one's rights as a citizen." "Democratic republics put the spirit of a court within reach of the multitude and let it penetrate through all classes at once." The result is a degradation of all citizens in a democracy, those in the majority as well as those who silently dissent from it, although Tocqueville says that the latter are much more corrupted than the former. This is so partly because the act of submission has the effect of nullifying whatever virtues the dissenters possessed. The corruption is heightened because all citizens in a democracy tend, to one extent or another, to acquiesce in the moral authority of the majority: Tocqueville says, "I know of only one way of preventing men from degrading themselves," and that way is not to allow the majority to become omnipotent. Yet, in general, the love of equality is stronger among human peoples than the love of independence.⁵⁵

In order to gauge the ability of Dewey's thought to avoid those four dangers, we should begin by discerning how Dewey would respond to Tocqueville's analysis of the principle of majority tyranny. Does Dewey teach that more "enlightenment and wisdom" are to be found in a large group of people than in a single person? His answer here is mixed: On the one hand, he never says that the larger the gathering is, the wiser it is. "A proposition does not gain validity because of the number of persons who accept it."⁵⁶ A group of two or three scientists may possess more wisdom than a "numerous assembly." On the other hand, there is a deep sense in which Dewey believes that no wisdom resides in a single person. We must distinguish here between the short run and the long run. In the short run, we may find much intelligence in an individual, even considered in isolation from others. But that intelligence has been acquired over time, Dewey insists, only through connections with other people; and if the individual is to remain intelligent, he must continue to associate with others. "Knowledge cooped up in a private consciousness is a myth" (*PIP*, 345).

Does Dewey teach that it is more important to maintain a certain number of legislators than to choose them in a certain way? He does not explicitly agree with this cause of majority omnipotence. But I do find an implicit agreement. Dewey's understanding of plural publics within a state would appear to call for a large number of legislators; for, as we have observed, although one representative may represent more than one interest, there would appear to be a limit to the number of interests that any one representative may effectively serve before a public decides that a larger number of representatives or a new institutional mechanism is necessary. Yet Dewey fails to give significant attention to the matter of selecting officials except to say that the manner is changeable, again demonstrating his greater concern with the end of democracy than with the means by which that end may be realized.

Does Dewey teach that politics should prefer the interest of the greatest number of people? Again I find a mixed answer in his writings. He disagrees with the view that an overall public welfare can be determined through "a summation of individuals quantitatively, similar to Bentham's purely quantitative formula of the greatest sum of pleasures of the greatest possible number." But he agrees with Bentham that the political standard is "the widest possible contribution to the interests of all—or at least of the great majority."[57] Dewey's use of the plural "interests" is perfectly consonant with his recognition of numerous public interests, and hence with his recognition of plural publics; the majority is not a permanent majority. Moreover, Dewey's use of the adjective "great" suggests that he is not an advocate of simple majority rule. How to secure the interests of the "great majority" remains, for him, an open question. He insists that there is no sanctity in majority rule as a means to that end (*PIP*, 326). But he finds it difficult to see how an alternative method could succeed in identifying the interests of the majority (*PIP*, 364). That alternative, it appears, would be to rely on a leader or leaders to identify the interests of the majority for them. Dewey's concern about the feasibility of this alternative is not so much the standard one that "each individual is the best judge of his own interests" as it is that only through discussion and persuasion, involving all members of a public, can its needs be ascertained.[58]

Let us turn now to the four main effects of majority omnipotence noted by Tocqueville. Would a Deweyan understanding of politics be able to prevent instability in legislation and administration? If we presume that political institutions will be ultimately responsive to the desires of groups of people, as Dewey does, then the answer to that question lies in the degree to which the wishes of publics will remain stable. Because of the existence of plural publics, and the possibility that their representatives might not be determined all at once in a single election, it is possible that this would not be such a problem for Dewey. Nor does Dewey attach any sanctity to frequent elections, which Tocqueville sees as an important cause of instability (*PIP*, 326). Yet because Dewey says that a good state is one that promotes liberty for its citizens and not merely prevents harm, we might expect to find constant demands from publics for action from the state—and in constantly changing situations too—thus tending toward instability.

We find an expression of concern from Dewey on the stability of human desire and thought in *Human Nature and Conduct;* we also find there, in his psychological theory, a very interesting possible solution. As we have noted, education involves the shaping of native human impulses through the formation of habits. An impulse may receive expression in three different ways. It may be released in "a surging, explosive discharge—blind, unintelligent." Alternatively, it may undergo "suppression," which is "the cause of all kinds of intellectual and moral pathology." But it may also be "sublimated—that is, become a factor coordinated intelligently with others in a continuing course of action. Thus a gust of anger may, because of its dynamic incorporation into disposition, be converted into an abiding conviction of social injustice to be remedied, and furnish the dynamic to carry the conviction into execution. . . . Such an outcome represents the normal or desirable functioning of impulse." Thus Dewey is hopeful that sublimation can happen often, but he hesitates to say definitively that it can normally be expected to happen. One reason for his hope is his intriguing suggestion that sublimation is susceptible or subject to rational control: when impulses are released, "it is the work of intelligence to find the ways of using them" (*HNC*, 108, 109, 118). This suggestion is surely contrary to psychoanalytic thinking. But it is certainly not out of the realm of possibility for us to consider, particularly given its broad agreement with work in the fields of rational-emotive therapy (by, e.g., Albert Ellis) and cognitive therapy.[59] The sublimation of impulses into "abiding convictions" would go a long way toward resolving the problem of legislative and administrative instability.[60]

Dewey is less successful, I believe, in offering a solution to the problem of arbitrarily used power. Yet it is also clearly a concern of his. The criterion for determining the worth of a state, he says, is not only "the degree of organization of the public which is attained" but also "the degree in which its officers are so constituted as to perform their function of caring for public interests" (*PIP*, 256). The maintenance of a state requires "constant watchfulness and criticism of public officials by citizens" (*PIP*, 278). Whatever changes in political machinery occur over time must be such as "to make the interest of the public a more supreme guide and criterion of governmental activity" (*PIP*, 327). The existence of plural publics, with the concomitant thought that in the final analysis public officials are kept in check not by a single, dominating majority but by numerous, differing groups, might have the effect of making each public more insistent that its representatives stay within clearly defined limits in such a complicated political world. Yet, with its emphasis on the experimental nature of constitutions and law, Dewey's theory all too easily gives publics a reason not to set definite limits on their administrators through law. This is so especially because, in his analysis of the nature of law in *The Public and Its Problems,* he rejects the view that laws are "commands" from a superior to an inferior; he believes that such a view ultimately involves reliance on something like a "general will" or an absolute reason. Instead Dewey teaches that laws are "structures which canalize action; they are active forces only as are banks which confine the flow of a stream, and are commands only in the sense in which the banks command the current" (*PIP*, 269). Laws do not define the terms of agreement among people but rather state the conditions within which people may decide upon the terms, or within which they may be able to determine the consequences of their acting or failing to act in a particular way. Thus laws are merely substitutes of predictability for a lack of human farsightedness (*PIP*, 270).

The existence of plural publics, which might to some extent mitigate the deleterious consequences of the first two problematic effects of majority tyranny noted, would likely not have that result concerning the last two: the maintenance of independence of thought and the avoidance of the "courtier spirit." The difficulty here is not that Dewey comes as close as he does to endorsing the principles lying behind the omnipotence of the majority. His insistence on the scientific method in education is testimony to his eagerness to see individuals have the resources to criticize judgments made by a majority. The question is whether he provides all of the resources necessary for the independence of citizens to exist. I suggest that he does not. The individual is so largely shaped by social forces that there is no, or hardly any, psychological room within which he may withdraw from society.[61] Moreover, Dewey sees the thought of the existence of any such room as a sign of a disruption in society in need of healing. His constant insistence in his educational thought on relating any and all activity to its social bearing would train a person to think that anything he does must have some value to another person in order to be worthwhile. "What is termed spiritual culture has usually been futile, with something rotten about it, just because it has been conceived as a thing which a man might have internally—and therefore exclusively" (*DE*, 129).

The prevalence of the "courtier spirit" means that no great—that is, strong or independent—characters can be found in a political society. Dewey's psychological and educational theories also suggest that such characters will be lacking among his publics. Surely it is not out of place to cite his understanding of the term "character" itself. At least twice he defines character in social terms: In 1916 he says that "character and mind are attitudes of participative response in social affairs" (*DE*, 326). In 1922 he writes, "Character is the interpenetration of habits," while habits are social functions and "interpenetration" means, in effect, harmonization. A "strong" character, in Dewey's view, is simply one where this "interpenetration" is "most marked," or where harmonization is closest to being "total" (*HNC*, 29, 30). If such is strength of character, where will the truly outstanding characters be in a Deweyan society? Again, there is no room to stand out, no room for truly individual genius to emerge or to form character.

In this chapter I have referred to Dewey's insistence on consultation and inquiry among the members of a public. "Communication" is the term he often uses, and it is surely a key notion in his political thought. Through communication "an order of energies" involving people or

things combined in action becomes an order of "meanings," necessary
if there is to be a true community "saturated and regulated by mutual
interest in shared meanings" (*PIP*, 331). Majority rule can operate successfully only with communication: "antecedent debates, modification
of views to meet the opinions of minorities, the relative satisfaction
given the latter by the fact that it has had a chance and that next time it
may be successful in becoming a majority" (*PIP*, 365). I shall explore
the notions of communication and meaning further in the next chapter,
along with Dewey's metaphysics; suffice it to say I do not think that
this emphasis on communication solves the problem of independence of
character. It is true that communication helps to develop individuality
of mind, but Dewey's thought seems unable to account for strong individuality itself.

TOCQUEVILLE VS. DEWEY ON LIBERTY

The conclusion that the points concerning independence of
thought and the courtier spirit lead toward is that Dewey's political theory fails in significant ways to provide adequately for liberty, at least as
Tocqueville understands liberty. A more direct comparison and contrast
of Dewey's and Tocqueville's understandings of liberty will also support
that conclusion. This juxtaposition is useful because, like Dewey, Tocqueville works with a positive conception of liberty instead of a negative
one.[62] Yet, as we shall see, Tocqueville's understanding of the relation
between the individual and society is very different from Dewey's.

For Tocqueville liberty is a certain character produced in citizens by
a number of factors. One is respect for law: Americans respect the law,
Tocqueville writes, not only because they are its source but also because
they feel "a sort of personal interest in obeying the laws, for a man who
is not today one of the majority party may be so tomorrow." Another
factor is an idea of rights, which aids us in steering a course between
license and tyranny; it teaches us to be "independent without arrogance
and obedient without servility." Finally, there is the relation of public
spirit to liberty. By "public spirit" Tocqueville means "patriotism," of
which he distinguishes two kinds: one the "instinctive love" of one's
homeland, the other a "more rational[,] . . . less generous, perhaps less
ardent, but more creative and more lasting" feeling that leads each per-

son to take part in local administration and thus to take a more general interest in public affairs.[63]

I have already mentioned Dewey's definition of liberty: it is "that secure release and fulfillment of personal potentialities which take place only in rich and manifold association with others" (*PIP*, 329). Dewey's understanding of liberty has elements of all three of the above factors that Tocqueville finds important. For Dewey, respect for law, when law is properly conceived, promotes rather than restricts liberty. An idea of rights is also crucial, as we have observed, but that idea must not be considered solely individualistic in nature: "As long as freedom of thought and speech is claimed as a merely individual right, it will give way, as do other merely personal claims, when it is, or is successfully represented to be, in opposition to the general welfare."[64] It must be seen as being in the interest of all that each citizen enjoy freedom of thought and speech. A concern with public spirit is seen primarily in Dewey's intent to show the harmony between self-interest and the welfare of the community through the championing of education in science, which furthers the democratic cause.

But on the matter of public spirit we find a key difference between Tocqueville and Dewey. Dewey subscribes wholeheartedly to what Tocqueville identifies as "the doctrine of self-interest properly understood": that it is "to the individual advantage of each to work for the good of all." Yet while Tocqueville shows how the doctrine is useful for fighting the influence of individualism, he does not say that it is simply true. We see that the doctrine is problematic for him in his analysis of "well-considered patriotism," which he says "is engendered by enlightenment, grows by the aid of laws and the exercise of rights, and in the end becomes, in a sense, mingled with personal interest." A love of one's country and one's fellow citizens may be given a start by education, but "in the end" personal interest must be appealed to in order for patriotism to be effective. Personal interest cannot be wholly encompassed or merged in "enlightenment" or the common good. Or, Tocqueville says, perhaps it is the individual's creative role—as creator of the general prosperity—to which the appeal must ultimately be made.[65] In the latter case, as Harvey C. Mansfield has suggested, we must combine interest with pride, or something like it, in order to arrive at a socially beneficial result.[66] In neither case do we find the identification of personal interest, enlightenment, and concern with the welfare of the community that we find in Dewey.

If there is an element of personal interest that cannot be captured in the doctrine of enlightened self-interest, as seems to me plausible, then something must be added to self-interest in order to tie the individual to society. This would indicate that there is a tension between individual and society, a gap that cannot be bridged by appeal to individual interest in the context of a "new individualism" as Dewey tries to do.

I suggest that any successful political liberalism must take account of three things. One of them is the possibility that the goods of all human beings may not be harmonizable. The second is one for which I have more esteem for Dewey: his recognition (along with Tocqueville) that the distinction between public and private is not etched in stone.[67] Early modern liberals such as Locke were aware of that too; but later, doctrinaire liberals have neglected it, applying more broadly such distinctions as Locke's between soul and body that he intended for a much narrower purpose.[68] It is very difficult to maintain the latter of those two facts, hence to maintain that we cannot concretely identify a private sphere to be guarded from political interference for all time, without forgetting the first of them. Dewey is able to take account of one, but not both, of those things.

Yet the maintenance of liberal democracy requires that we remember both facts. We must remember the possibility of the irreconcilability of human goods in order to encourage the prevention of tyranny and slavery in its various forms as much as possible. We must remember the shifting ground underlying any distinction between public and private, for one reason, so that we do not have the government forswear any concern with human character, as many (but certainly not all) liberals desire today, and for another reason, so that we do not overemphasize the possibility of the irreconcilability of human goods.

Nevertheless—and here is the third, paradoxical fact—the stability of liberal democracy also demands more of a fixed principle of separation between private and public than recognition of that shifting ground would indicate. The rule of laws and not of men still appears to suit us best; it follows that we must draw a line between public and private sharper than what seems philosophically justifiable. Is our age too enlightened to live with that tension?

Is it true that a degree of self-centeredness, sufficient to prevent a complete harmonization of the individual with society, is natural to humans? Dewey's denial of that claim depends not only on his psychology and ethics, but also on his metaphysics. In fact his entire defense of democracy is closely tied to the core of his metaphysics. It is therefore necessary that we consider in detail the relation of Dewey's political theory to his metaphysics.

NOTES

1. Walter Lippmann, *The Phantom Public* (New York: Macmillan, 1925), 126.
2. John Dewey, review of *Public Opinion* by Walter Lippmann (1922), in M13 (1983): 339, 344.
3. John Dewey, "Practical Democracy" (1925), in L2:219.
4. Alan Ryan fails to see that Dewey's understanding of the purpose of the state is not the typical pluralist view—i.e., the arbitration of conflicts, the prevention of harm—when he writes, "Dewey's picture of the role and purpose of government makes it essentially an enterprise for mopping up the negative consequences that our voluntary actions may have for strangers and facilitating our avoidance of bad side effects that we may not have noticed and that will cause us trouble in future." Ryan, *Dewey and American Liberalism,* 218. Avigail Eisenberg also misrepresents Dewey's view of the state as "a set of neutral instruments." Avigail I. Eisenberg, *Reconstructing Political Pluralism* (Albany: State University of New York Press, 1995), 68.
5. John Locke, *Second Treatise of Government,* secs. 96, 134, 212 (quotation from 212; italics in original). Compare Thomas Hobbes, *Leviathan,* chap. 29. Whereas Hobbes identifies civil society with the commonwealth or state and represents the commonwealth in the legal "person" of the sovereign or government, Locke clearly distinguishes between civil society and government.
6. Georg W. F. Hegel, *Philosophy of Right,* trans. T. M. Knox (London: Oxford University Press, 1952), paragraphs 75, 100.
7. Ibid., paragraphs 157, 182.
8. Pierre Hassner, "Georg W. F. Hegel," trans. Allan Bloom, in *History of Political Philosophy,* 3d ed., ed. Leo Strauss and Joseph Cropsey (Chicago: University of Chicago Press, 1987), 743.
9. Locke, *Second Treatise,* secs. 129, 149.
10. Ibid., sec. 134 (both phrases italicized in original).
11. John Locke, *Some Thoughts Concerning Education,* sec. 115.
12. Peter Laslett, note to sec. 16 of *Second Treatise,* in John Locke, *Two*

Treatises of Government, ed. Peter Laslett (Cambridge: Cambridge University Press, 1988), 278 (italics added).

13. Locke, *Second Treatise,* secs. 7, 6 (both phrases italicized in original).

14. Ibid., sec. 123 (italics in original). Locke mentions preservation as the purpose of government numerous times, whereas only once in the *Second Treatise* does he say that "the increase of lands and the right imploying of them is the great art of government" (sec. 42). Whether "preservation" requires "increase" is an interesting question.

15. John Dewey, "Does Human Nature Change?" (1938), in L13 (1988): 286–87.

16. John Dewey, "Ethical Principles Underlying Education" (1897), in E5 (1972): 60, 55, 57.

17. John Dewey, *Individualism, Old and New* (1930), in L5 (1984): 67.

18. The one statement contrary to this tenor that I can find in Dewey's writing is in *The Public and Its Problems:* "I would not say" that individuals "have no point nor sense except in some combination" (*PIP,* 278). But contrast a statement made later: the individual "is a value in potential humanity and not as something separate and atomic." John Dewey, "The Basic Values and Loyalties of Democracy" (1941), in L14:277.

19. John Dewey, "I Believe" (1939), in L14:91, 92. See also "Creative Democracy—The Task Before Us" (1939), in L14:227: the "heart and final guarantee of democracy" are freedom of press and assembly.

20. Dewey, "Ethical Principles," 64, 65.

21. John Dewey, *Democracy and Education* (1916), in M9 (1980): 129, 132. Hereafter I shall refer to this work parenthetically in the text as *DE* followed by page number. See also, e.g., "Authority and Social Change" (1936), in L11:136; *The Dewey School,* Appendix 2 (1936), in L11:204; "A Liberal Speaks Out for Liberalism" (1936), in L11:288; *Experience and Education* (1938), in L13.

22. Dewey, "I Believe," 91, 92.

23. John Dewey, "Presenting Thomas Jefferson" (1940), in L14:212.

24. John Dewey, "Liberalism and Civil Liberties" (1936), in L11:374.

25. John Dewey, *Liberalism and Social Action* (1935), in L11:26, 40, 30, 50.

26. Hegel, *Philosophy of Right,* paragraph 324.

27. See Karl Marx, *On the Jewish Question, Manifesto of the Communist Party* (the latter work with Friedrich Engels).

28. Aristotle, *Politics,* 1280a7–81a7.

29. Jean-Jacques Rousseau, *Discourse on Political Economy,* in *The Collected Writings of Rousseau,* vol. 3, ed. Roger D. Masters and Christopher Kelly, trans. Judith R. Bush, Roger D. Masters, Christopher Kelly, and Terence Marshall (Hanover, N.H.: University Press of New England, 1992), esp. 148, 152, 154–57, 164–65 (quotation from 154).

30. Locke, *Second Treatise,* sec. 13.

31. Whether the focus would remain strictly on the commonalities is a question I take up later.

32. The other cases would be those where a transaction between private individuals presents the opportunity for the advancement of the welfare of others. Recall that Dewey sets no limit to the scope of the state.

33. John Dewey, "Internal Social Reorganization after the War" (1918), in M11 (1982): 83.

34. See, e.g., Westbrook, *Dewey and American Democracy,* 317.

35. Dewey, "Internal Social Reorganization"; "What Are We Fighting For?" (1918), in M11; "I Believe."

36. Dewey, "What Are We Fighting For?" 105.

37. John Dewey, "No Half-Way House for America" (1934), in L9:289–90. Alan Ryan is thus partially incorrect to suggest that Dewey is "not particularly socialist if by 'socialist' we mean attaching great importance to public ownership and the abolition of private property in the means of production." Ryan, *Dewey and American Liberalism,* 88. Dewey does attach importance to public ownership, although he never calls for a total end to private property as a productive force.

38. John Dewey and James H. Tufts, *Ethics,* 2d ed. (1932), in L7 (1985): 363. I am unable to tell whether Dewey or Tufts wrote this passage (as opposed to the first edition of 1908, where the authors make clear in the preface who wrote which parts), and I assume that both authors take responsibility for the entire work.

39. In Steiner's *Rethinking Democratic Education* the judging of rhetoric is a central activity of citizens.

40. John Dewey, *Human Nature and Conduct* (1922), in M14 (1983): 31, 32, 16. Hereafter I shall refer to this work parenthetically in the text as *HNC* followed by page number.

41. John Dewey, *Freedom and Culture* (1939), in L13:135. Hereafter I shall refer to this work parenthetically in the text as *FC* followed by page number. See also *DE,* 232–39.

42. For identification of the following quotations and for comments, I am indebted to electronic mail from Craig A. Cunningham on the John Dewey discussion list (15 February 1996, dewey-l@postoffice.cso.uiuc.edu).

43. John Dewey, *Art as Experience* (1934), in L10 (1987): 286. Hereafter I shall refer to this work parenthetically in the text as *AE* followed by page number.

44. John Dewey, "Progressive Education and the Science of Education" (1928), in L3 (1984): 263.

45. Alasdair MacIntyre, *After Virtue,* 2d ed. (Notre Dame, Ind.: University of Notre Dame Press, 1984), 263.

46. Michael J. Sandel, *Liberalism and the Limits of Justice* (Cambridge: Cambridge University Press, 1982), 172.

47. Eisenberg, *Reconstructing Political Pluralism,* 40–53.

48. See Michael Walzer, *Spheres of Justice* (New York: Basic Books, 1983).

49. See Michael J. Sandel, "America's Search for a New Public Philosophy," *Atlantic Monthly,* March 1996, 57–74. The one contrary note of which I am aware is Sandel's statement that "communitarians would be more likely than liberals to allow a town to ban pornographic bookstores, on the grounds that pornography offends its way of life and the values that sustain it." Michael J. Sandel, "Morality and the Liberal Ideal," *New Republic,* 7 May 1984, 17.

50. See, e.g., Joseph G. Metz, "Democracy and the Scientific Method in the Philosophy of John Dewey," *Review of Politics* 31 (April 1969): 254.

51. Alexis de Tocqueville, *Democracy in America,* ed. J. P. Mayer, trans. George Lawrence (Garden City, N.Y.: Anchor, 1969), 246, 247.

52. Ibid., 248–50.

53. Ibid., 253–54.

54. Ibid., 254–56.

55. Ibid., 257–59, 57.

56. John Dewey, *Logic: The Theory of Inquiry* (1938), in L12 (1986): 484n4.

57. Dewey, *Liberalism and Social Action,* 50, 56.

58. For Tocqueville that "standard" individualistic principle is the idea behind life in the communitarian organization of the American township. Tocqueville, *Democracy in America,* 66.

59. I am grateful to Christopher Heavey and Terry Knapp for discussion on this point.

60. Whether "an abiding conviction of social injustice" is the most sublime outlet for a sublimated impulse can be doubted.

61. I do not see how John Patrick Diggins can say, "Dewey had no use for Tocqueville and hence could not bring himself to see the mind as more the creature than the creator of social forces." Diggins, *Promise of Pragmatism,* 379. First, as Dewey makes clear in *Human Nature and Conduct,* among other works, he believes precisely the opposite about the human mind: "the natural unaided mind means precisely the habits of belief, thought and desire which have been accidentally generated and confirmed by social institutions or customs. But with all their admixture of accident and reasonableness we have at last reached a point where social conditions create a mind capable of scientific outlook and inquiry" (*HNC,* 225–26). Second, as I am attempting to show in this chapter, Dewey's rejection of Tocqueville, although significant, is far from total.

62. I rely on the distinction made most famously by Sir Isaiah Berlin, *Two Concepts of Liberty* (Oxford: Oxford University Press, Clarendon Press, 1958).

63. Tocqueville, *Democracy in America,* 235–40.

64. Dewey, *Liberalism and Social Action,* 47. Here is, I think, Dewey's strongest step toward a notion of group rights that would complement, if not substitute for, individual rights. Yet he does not develop it beyond this point.

65. Tocqueville, *Democracy in America,* 525, 235–36.

66. Harvey C. Mansfield, "Self-Interest Rightly Understood," *Political Theory* 23 (February 1995): 62–63.

67. For an interesting treatment of this point see James W. Ceaser, *Liberal Democracy and Political Science* (Baltimore: Johns Hopkins University Press, 1990), 33–40.

68. See John Locke, *A Letter Concerning Toleration.*

3

DEWEY'S JUSTIFICATION OF DEMOCRACY

As we clarify the relation of Dewey's political theory to his meta-physics, we shall also clarify Dewey's thought by examining its relation to postmodernism. Postmodernism, with its rejection of philo-sophical foundations for politics such as natural right or natural law—its rejection of what Richard Rorty has called "foundationalism"—has no universally accepted history. Some point to Nietzsche as the first post-modernist, others to Heidegger, others to Wittgenstein or Derrida. On the question of foundationalism Dewey, as I shall show, seems to belong both to the philosophical tradition and to the sort of opposition to the tradition that is found in Rorty.[1] According to Rorty, "Dewey thought of himself as freeing us up for practice, not as providing theoretical foun-dations for practice."[2] Richard Bernstein, however, has maintained that Dewey's concern is "to articulate, texture, and *justify* a vision of a prag-matically viable ideal of communal democracy."[3] Who is correct?

Dewey wrote dozens of books and hundreds of articles, but none of them is singularly devoted to providing an answer to the question of justification. This fact might lead one to conclude that the question is not important for him, that he sees democracy as so evidently the only proper form of government that further discussion is unnecessary. This possibility is certainly worth considering, for in order to understand Dewey we must try to grasp his concerns and not be guided by our own, which may be foreign to him. His work, however, shows that he does not consider the question of grounding democracy trivial. One of his chief concerns is with showing that our ideals and forms of associa-tion have more than just a subjective standing—a concern typical of foundationalist thinkers.

Even as philosophers and others most often use the terms "moral subjectivism" or "conventionalism"—to refer to the view that no moral standard can be found independent of human opinion—Dewey wants to stand opposed to it. Two of Dewey's works are noteworthy here. First, in *The Quest for Certainty,* one of his most radical books, he objects to a brand of empiricism that identifies goodness with emotional satisfaction, on the ground that it "holds down value to objects *antecedently* enjoyed, apart from reference to the method by which they come into existence. . . . Operational thinking needs to be applied to the judgment of values just as it has now finally been applied in conceptions of physical objects."[4] He continues, "The formation of a cultivated and effectively operative good judgment or taste with respect to what is esthetically admirable, intellectually acceptable and morally approvable is the supreme task set to human beings by the incidents of experience" (*QC,* 209). Second, in the revised edition of his textbook *Ethics* (written with James H. Tufts), he rebuts John Stuart Mill's claim in *Utilitarianism* that "the sole evidence it is possible to produce that anything is desirable is that people do actually desire it" by asserting that it would be "stupid to assume that what *should* be desired can be determined by a mere examination of what men do desire, until a critical examination of the *reasonableness* of things desired has taken place. So there is a distinction between the enjoy*ed* and the enjoy*able*."[5]

At times, however, Dewey very much like a moral subjectivist. For example, he seems to contradict blatantly his claim concerning Mill when he writes, "Things are valuable when they are valued; that is, when they are esteemed and chosen. . . . Want, effort, and choice are more fundamental concepts than value."[6] It requires an examination of Dewey's teaching to see that, while this passage could have been better worded, there is not simply a ridiculous inconsistency here. Let it suffice here to say that Dewey does not always speak of "subjectivism" in the most common way. I shall try to show his project in now turning to the particular question set for this chapter.

THE BEGINNINGS OF DEWEY'S DEFENSE OF DEMOCRACY

Dewey holds that the most important aspect of democracy is not political. Indeed, as early as 1888, when he was still a philosophical idealist, Dewey used the word "democracy" to mean something more than a form of government. Writing in refutation of Sir Henry Maine, who had claimed in his book *Popular Government* that it is nothing more, Dewey argues that democracy is "an ethical conception, and upon its ethical significance is based its significance as governmental."[7] Twenty years later he says that democratic government is merely "the effective embodiment of the moral ideal of a good which consists in the development of all the social capacities of every individual member of society."[8] The sort of society required for this development is one "where there is a wide and varied distribution of opportunities; where there is social mobility or scope for change of position and station; where there is free circulation of experiences and ideas, making for a wide recognition of common interests and purposes, and where utility of social and political organization to its members is so obvious as to enlist their warm and constant support in its behalf."[9] This "free circulation" cannot be limited to only certain spheres of life if democracy is to be fully realized. "To be realized it must affect all modes of human association, the family, the school, industry, religion" (*PIP*, 325).

Dewey has been criticized (and the preceding two quotations, taken together and in isolation, certainly lend themselves to such attack) for providing a theoretical basis for the permissiveness that is widely regarded to have resulted from the progressive movement in education. However justified this criticism may be, it has often been exaggerated. Dewey defends the existence of figures of authority in such institutions as the school; he wrote *Experience and Education* for this purpose.[10] Nor, as we saw in the previous chapter, does Dewey defend pure democracy to the point of attacking representative government. What democracy requires as a moral ideal is that "the supreme test of all political institutions and industrial arrangements [indeed, he says elsewhere, of all institutions] shall be the contribution they make to the all-around growth of every member of society."[11] "Growth" is a very important word for Dewey, as we shall see shortly.

What conditions does this requirement impose on politics? One of Dewey's chief objections to Marxism is that it sanctions undemocratic means for egalitarian ends, so he might be expected to hold that certain political arrangements, in broad features, are indispensable for the "growth" of each person.[12] Indeed, while he has no permanent attachment to any particular political institution, he says that "experience has shown" that universal suffrage, in general, and "direct participation in choice of rulers," in particular, are essential to sound government.[13] Twenty years later, in his most concise statement on democracy, "Democracy and Educational Administration," he elaborates:

> The political and governmental phase of democracy is a means, the best means so far found, for realizing ends that lie in the wide domain of human relationships and the development of human personality. . . .
>
> Universal suffrage, recurring elections, responsibility of those who are in political power to the voters, and the other factors of democratic government are means that have been found expedient for realizing democracy as the truly human way of living. They are not a final end and a final value. They are to be judged on the basis of their contribution to end.[14]

The arrangements of democratic politics, then, are justified on the grounds of their promotion of the broader democratic ideal.

Why is that ideal choiceworthy? One way of putting Dewey's answer is that moral democracy entails "growth," which is "the only moral 'end' " (*RP,* 181). "Not perfection as a final goal, but the ever-enduring process of perfecting, maturing, refining is the aim in living." One scholar of Dewey put the point well in noting that for Dewey "growth" provides "a relativistic understanding of human development within a universalistic framework."[15]

Our next question is: How do we distinguish growth from its opposite? If Dewey's notion is relativistic, we should not conclude that it is completely dependent upon conditions. Dewey does offer guidance as to what may constitute growth. We have already noted his use of phrases such as "distribution of opportunities," "social mobility," "free circulation of experiences." In *Democracy and Education* Dewey states two important criteria in the form of questions: if we want to know the worth of a form of association, we need to ask, "How numerous and varied are the interests which are consciously shared? How full and free is the interplay with other forms of association?" (*DE,* 89). The greater the number and variety of shared interests, and the fuller and freer the interaction among different groups, the more developed those interests and groups are. The members of a criminal organization may share only one, limited interest, and their opportunities for candid interaction with other groups are highly restricted. Dewey would say that such a group offers little or no possibility for growth and could thus not be part of a workable democracy.

In further response to the question of the choiceworthiness of the moral ideal of democracy, many who share Dewey's belief that the democratic spirit should infuse all areas of life might be expected to appeal to a general faith in human nature; and it is commonly thought that Dewey shares this faith. He encourages this opinion at two points, at least. First, in an article containing one of his few explicit assertions of the grounds for democratic government, he contrasts autocracy and democracy. Whereas the enforced uniformity of autocracy strains human nature, democracy "releases and relieves it—such, I take it, is the ultimate sanction of democracy."[16] Second, democratic political arrangements "rest back upon the idea that no man or limited set of men is wise enough or good enough to rule others without their consent."[17]

Dewey's full answer to the question is not so simple, however. As I have noted, in an article distinguishing his liberalism from that of natural rights, he credits Oliver Wendell Holmes and Louis D. Brandeis for their willingness to ground their defense of liberalism on the social value of free inquiry and discussion, rather than on "anything inherent in the individual as such." He makes his position clearer in "Democracy and Educational Administration": "The foundation of democracy is faith in the capacities of human nature; faith in human intelligence, and in the power of pooled and cooperative experience. It is not belief that these things are complete but that if given a show they will grow and be able to generate progressively the knowledge and wisdom needed to guide collective action."[18]

What then exactly does Dewey mean by "human nature"? Is there nothing inherent in the individual worth trusting? On this subject he observes, "The supposition that there is such a thing as a purely native original constitution of man which can be distinguished from everything acquired and learned cannot be justified by appeal to the facts."[19] This answer is not tantamount to saying there is nothing inherent in the individual at all. In a later article he addresses "the innate needs of men" and writes, "I do not think it can be shown that" they "have changed since man became man" or that they will change.[20] These needs are "the inherent demands that men make because of their constitution [for example, food, drink, movement]. . . . There are other things not so directly physical that seem to me equally engrained in human nature." As examples he gives needs for companionship, for aesthetic expression, even for combat. He adds, however, that we err when we think "that the manifestation of these needs is also unalterable."[21] Instincts arising from these needs are susceptible to the influence of social conditions. For instance, war exists because social forces have channeled the need and instinct for combat in a base direction. To those who should object that certain emotions are so fundamental to humans and so specific in a given moral direction that certain manifestations are inevitable, Dewey would reply that an emotion is not a psychic state that can be located in a given individual. What most people call mental states, Dewey terms "qualities" of "organic reactions" or of a "situation of experience."[22]

Those last words in quotation marks are central to Dewey's comprehensive philosophy, and to his major work on metaphysics, *Experience and Nature*. In order to follow the trail of Dewey's social and political theory further, we need to turn for a while to other aspects of his philosophy.

DEWEY'S NOTION OF CONTINUITY

If the term "experience" is taken as it is normally used, to mean something that goes on strictly within an individual, then Dewey will be misunderstood. At the beginning of *Experience and Nature,* however, he pretty clearly objects to this reading: experience is not "a veil or screen which shuts us off from nature."[23] Not always (he also uses the term in the usual, subjective sense), but typically, "experience" for Dewey includes both individual and nature—or, to use two of Dewey's common expressions, "organism" and "environment"—which are often set in philosophical opposition to each other. A "situation," in Dewey's account, is a transaction between organism and environment.

The fundamental contention of *Experience and Nature* is that of continuity—between experience (here intended subjectively) and nature, mind and world. Dewey writes in the preface to the second edition, "The isolation of nature and experience from each other has rendered the undeniable connection of thought and effectiveness of knowledge and purposive action, with the body, an insoluble mystery. Restoration of continuity is shown to do away with the mind-body problem" (*EN*, 7–8). He concludes the preface, "The chief obstacle to a more effective criticism of current values lies in the traditional separation of nature and experience, which it is the purpose of this volume to replace by the idea of continuity" (*EN*, 9).

But while "continuity" is one of the key terms in Dewey's philosophy in general and metaphysics in particular, it is also one of the most difficult to pin down, even within the context of *Experience and Nature.*[24] Pragmatism—or, as Dewey prefers to call it, instrumentalism—emerged as a philosophical attempt to explain mental conduct in a way capable of empirical verification.[25] Thus, if Dewey is to have a metaphysics within the bounds of his experimentalism, it must be a "naturalistic metaphysics"—one, that is, that pertains generally to things in the natural world. Dewey says that the goal of metaphysics is "detection and description of the generic traits of existence" (*EN*, 52). By "generic traits of existence" Dewey means the characteristics or qualities shared by all existences, and he gives examples: "[T]he significant problems and issues of life and philosophy concern the rate and mode of the conjunction of the precarious and the assured, the incomplete and the finished, the repetitious and the varying, the safe and sane and the hazardous. If we trust to the evidence of experienced things, these traits, and the modes and tempos of their interaction with each other, are fundamental features of natural existence" (*EN*, 66–67). He continues, "Structure and process, substance and accident, matter and energy, permanence and flux, one and many, continuity and discreteness, order and progress, law and liberty, uniformity and growth, tradition and innovation, rational will and impelling desires, proof and discovery, the actual and the possible, are names given to various phases of their conjunction, and the issue of living depends upon the art with which these things are adjusted to each other" (*EN*, 67). Dewey here clearly identifies continuity as among the generic traits of existence. As S. Morris Eames states, "The fullness of experience envelops the generic traits of existence, traits of stability and instability, order and disorder, harmony and disharmony, continuity and discontinuity."[26] When Dewey speaks of traits of existence, he usually brings up polarities such as continuity and discreteness, precariousness and stability, and suggests that existences can be placed on a sliding scale between two opposites.

Later in *Experience and Nature*, Dewey elaborates on the meaning of continuity and discreteness. "Existentially speaking," he writes, "a human individual is distinctive opacity of bias and preference conjoined with plasticity and permeability of needs and likings. One trait tends to isolation, discreteness; the other trait to connection, continuity" (*EN,* 186). "Discreteness" and "continuity" are "rooted in nature," he says, but they "persist upon the human plane." Each human being is unique, yet he can reach out to others; the latter ability assumes continuity. Thus "continuity" for Dewey involves connection of organism and environment. I shall subsequently refer to continuity in this sense as a(n existential) *continuum* between organism and environment.

In writing of continuity as continuum in *Experience and Nature,* Dewey elaborates on an earlier writing: eight years before the first edition of *Experience and Nature* he says that existence is characterized by "active bonds or continuities of all kinds, together with static discontinuities."[27] Ten years after the second edition of *Experience and Nature* he says that the environment is "marked by both discreteness and continuity."[28]

In *Experience and Nature* Dewey writes that experience "recognizes in its primary integrity no division between act and material, subject and object, but contains them both in an unanalyzed totality" (*EN,* 18). Perhaps more than any other, that sentence invites the conclusion that continuum is equivalent to identity, that everything is the same as everything else. Yet the "totality" is such only insofar as it is considered in its "primary integrity," only insofar as it is "unanalyzed"; if all things were the same thing they could be analyzed—distinguished from one another—only in an illusory way.[29]

Continuity does not have only the sense of continuum in Dewey's thought. It also figures in Dewey's work on logic, in a different but related sense. His explanation of the term there is worth quoting at length:

> The term "naturalistic" has many meanings. As it is here employed it means, on one side, that there is no breach of continuity between operations of inquiry and biological operations and physical operations. "Continuity," on the other side, means that rational operations *grow out of* organic activities, without being identical with that from which they emerge. . . .
>
> The primary postulate of a naturalistic theory of logic is continu-

ity of the lower (less complex) and the higher (more complex) activities and forms. The idea of continuity is not self-explanatory. But its meaning excludes complete rupture on one side and mere repetition of identities on the other; it precludes the reduction of the "higher" to the "lower" just as it precludes complete breaks and gaps. The growth and development of any living organism from seed to maturity illustrates the meaning of continuity.[30]

Thus here, in a second sense, continuity means the *growth or development* of an organism.[31] Elsewhere, Dewey refers more generally to "continuity of the life process" through "the renewal of physical existence" (*DE*, 4, 5).

What sense of continuity Dewey has in mind at a particular place is not always easy to determine. Nor is it always easy to figure what he sees as the relation between continuity as continuum and continuity as growth. For example, in *Human Nature and Conduct* he writes, "A morals based on study of human nature instead of upon disregard for it would find the facts of man continuous with those of the rest of nature and would thereby ally ethics with physics and biology" (*HNC*, 11). Does he here mean to speak of the continuum between man and nature, or of the growth or emergence of man from natural processes? Perhaps he has both in mind. Thomas Alexander provides a possible link between the two senses by suggesting that for Dewey "continuity refers to increasing levels of organic functioning which exclude either the possibility of being reduced to one identical type or of being utterly disconnected into self-enclosed, autonomous categories."[32]

Without disagreeing with Alexander, one could argue that for Dewey continuity in the sense of continuum is a precondition or presupposition of continuity in the sense of growth. Without a continuum between organism and environment, how an organism can grow from its interactions with its environment would be inexplicable, because the more basic question of how an organism can interact with its environment would be inexplicable. The perception of discontinuities in nature, or lack of growth and development, depends on the existence of continuity in the sense of continuum. As H. S. Thayer notes,

> Continuity is seen [by Dewey] as a deeper and more pervasive trait of things [than conflict or discontinuity]; indeed, it underlies or is a

feature of conflict. For the conflict that initiates human deliberation and inquiry is itself "continuous" with conditions (material, organic, and social) that precede it and with those that are to follow. For Dewey, the occurrences of conflicts and tensions in general have a natural history; they do not arise *ex nihilo*. And that history, whatever its specific characteristics may be, like all histories, exhibits continuity.[33]

Taken together, those two senses of continuity yield Dewey's principle of continuity. Continuity is a principle essential for overcoming numerous traditional philosophical problems, according to Dewey. These problems, he believes, can be traced ultimately to false dualisms. To take probably the most fundamental example, if we are given a mind internal to a person on one side and an external world (including the body connected to that mind—hence the "mind-body problem") on the other, how can the mind hook up with the world to find out about it? If, however, "mind" and "world" are not conceived of as existentially separate, but instead as analytical terms of distinction, functional discriminations from an original totality, then the problem dissolves. Knowledge is something that occurs, and we may usefully describe it as an activity in terms such as "mind" and "world," as long as we do not distort their significance.

It is clear that continuity plays a fundamental, indispensable role in Dewey's thought. I would argue that it makes most sense to understand continuity as both a presupposition and a conclusion of Dewey's metaphysics—in other words, as both a regulative idea or principle and a generic trait of existence. It is a presupposition because it is needed to explain the precondition for metaphysical inquiry. As a presupposition, continuity in the sense of continuum between organism and environment is always present. It is a conclusion because continuity is not always fully present in existences; things are discrete as well as connected to one another.[34] To say that it is a presupposition or regulative principle of Dewey's metaphysics, however, is not to imply that it is an absolute assumption for him or that he never offers reasons for the doctrine of continuity. We shall examine the status of continuity later.

DEWEY'S DEFENSE OF DEMOCRACY CONTINUED

When we left Dewey's political theory, we were attempting to determine what he thinks of human nature. Not only is continuity a key to understanding Dewey's so-called "faith in human nature"—the subject that led us to the topic of continuity—it is the cornerstone of the entire radical philosophical project that lies behind that faith, including the problem of moral objectivity. Dewey took to heart as much as anyone else an evolutionary view of the universe; indeed he saw it as one of the metaphysical implications of pragmatism.[35] One reason for his inability to accept the Cartesian notion of truth as correspondence between idea and object is that he does not see objects as holding still long enough to be grasped by the mind. If truth is neither correctly copying the "external" world nor an "internal" creation of the mind, what is possible but some cooperation between the two? Thus Dewey says that it is not "the object alone which decides what is the proper and authorized account of itself; but the object as a term and factor in established social practice."[36] Moreover, since ideals do not inhabit a separate realm from nature, yet have certain effects in nature when acted upon, claims of virtue and vice "can be studied as objectively as physiological functions," and in the same way: by the method of modern science (*HNC,* 16).

What exactly does he mean by "objectively"? He reveals the answer when he considers "the old question of the objectivity or subjectivity of morals" (*HNC,* 38). What we see, however, is that "the old question"—Is there a moral standard independent of human opinion?—is transformed into a new one. "Primarily," Dewey says, morals "are objective. For will, . . . means, in the concrete, habits; and habits incorporate an environment within themselves. They are adjustments *of* the environment, not merely *to* it." Habits may conflict with one another, however. "Life, for example, involves the habit of eating, which in turn involves a unification of organism and nature. But nevertheless this habit comes into conflict with other habits which are also 'objective,' or in equilibrium with *their* environments. . . . Honor or consideration for others or courtesy conflicts with hunger. Then the notion of the complete objectivity of morals gets a shock" (*HNC,* 38–39). Some people are led to reject "natural morality" and resort to "transcendentalism" because aims often conflict, but Dewey's task is "to see what objectivity signifies upon a naturalistic basis; how morals are objective and yet secular and social. Then we may be able to decide in what crisis of experience morals become legitimately dependent upon character or self—that is, 'subjective' " (*HNC,* 39). He goes on to explain that ideals can be

legitimately subjective where conditions prevent their immediate fulfillment but where they work through habits eventually to secure themselves between the organism and the environment.

It is clear, then, that in Dewey's scheme "objective" is applied to
morals having to do with transactions between the organism and the
environment, while "subjective" pertains to those having to do with the
organism considered in isolation. The old dichotomy has taken on a
new meaning. Dewey is not being disingenuous here when he speaks of
"the old question"; in numerous writings prior to this one he has considered and criticized the traditional dichotomy, and it is safe to assume
that here he phrases that question in the only form he thinks legitimate
or meaningful. What I do want to establish is that, for Dewey, human
purposes, as they are at a given time, are properly an ingredient in the
determination of good and bad. He makes this point very clear when he
writes, "In as far as the subjectivity of modern thought represents a
discovery of the part played by personal responses, organic and acquired,
in the causal production of the qualities and values of objects, it marks
the possibility of a decisive gain" (*QC,* 220–21).

As we saw in the previous chapter, Dewey's notion of scientific
method consists, in outline, of perplexity, hypothesis, survey, elaboration
of hypothesis, and test of hypothesis. In that rough form, it may be
applied outside the laboratory—and, Dewey claims, to problems not
traditionally called scientific. Scientific and ethical judgments are logi-
cally equivalent, he says, for the origin and purpose of the former lie in
unique cases, and the latter "require for their control generic propositions, which state a connection of relevant conditions in universal (or
objective) form."[37] "Purely objectively, there is no reason for choosing
any one of the infinite possibilities [for subject of judgment] rather than
another."[38] All scientific propositions are normative, as their worth is
determined by their ability to regulate descriptions; all are moral, in
that they are the result of individual interests. Of course, Dewey is not
proposing that human beings be subjected to the same sort of treatment
given to inanimate objects, but he is insisting that the experimental *attitude,* especially the quality of tentativeness, that has proven successful in
dealing with the natural world be applied to social and political problems
as well.

To those who appeal to natural right or natural law, Dewey's position on applying scientific method to ethics might seem dangerously

close to subjectivism or conventionalism. Dewey, however, asserts a link between natural right and subjectivism.

> [T]he implication of placing the standard of thought and knowledge in antecedent existence is that our thought makes no difference in what is significantly real. It then affects only our own attitude toward it.
>
> This constant throwing of emphasis back upon a change made in ourselves instead of one made in the world in which we live seems to me the essence of what is objectionable in "subjectivism." Its taint hangs about even Platonic realism with its insistent evangelical dwelling upon the change made within the mind by contemplation of the realm of essence. (*QC*, 219)

When we look to nature for our standard of conduct, we are forced to dwell upon ourselves in order to be sure we have the standard right and thereby seclude ourselves from the world. Progress in natural inquiry began to come when humans dismissed the notion of natural teleology; and since ends must come from somewhere, it is inevitable that human purposes be a factor in knowledge (*RP*, 116–19).

We are now in a position to explain the apparent discrepancy between Dewey's criticism of John Stuart Mill and his statement, "Things are valuable when they are valued." Dewey does not mean that whatever is valued is truly of worth. For him a thing *can* be valuable only when it is valued—when it is taken as something of worth in a specific situation, as a factor in valuation. Values are not found in nature alone, apart from human purposes. Whatever is not valued is not necessarily worthless; it may be "invaluable," a description of certain things "outside the sphere of valuation [i.e., at the present time]."[39] Instead of the statement above, Dewey should have written (and it is generous to think he meant) that things can be valuable only when valued.

Dewey has a ready reply to the critic who charges him with simple conventionalism: Unlike conventionalists, he does not give wholehearted approval to human purposes as they are at a given time. First, the purpose that is taken for granted in determining the worth of a certain action must itself be prepared to submit to inquiry to determine its worth. Second, no judgment about a purpose is to be taken as settled once and for all; indeed any conclusion in any field of inquiry must be accepted tentatively. Thus Dewey prefers the phrase "warranted assertibility" to "truth."[40]

Yet how do we know that modern science has made the progress over Aristotelian science that enables us to judge it superior, if its conclusions are subject to revision? Determining the worth of a purpose is not an easy assignment. The dilemma seems all the graver when we read Dewey's answer to the following question: If a purpose, or in hardened form a custom, is the starting point of all inquiry into things, where do we turn when we doubt a custom? "We cannot recur to objects just as they present themselves, for these objects are thoroughly infected with the influence of just those customs which have become suspected."[41]

Here, there can be no doubt, Dewey resorts to a faith in the scientific method—but this statement must be qualified. The experimental method, Dewey says, is "unbiased" (*RP*, 108). Yet its conclusions must always be accepted tentatively. If its conclusions must always be accepted tentatively, how can we be sure it is unbiased? The only solution possible to Dewey is to say that we have faith that, *over time,* science comes to deal successfully with natural events happening around us (and Dewey does not deny the existence of things and events prior to and independent of human awareness, though he is not interested in them if they cannot be brought into experience, experience taken as transaction between organism and environment). Nature is in fact "empirically disclosed (by the use of empirical method in natural science)," but we can be sure of this fact only over a period of time (*EN,* 11). We can now see the limited extent to which Dewey accepts some form of the correspondence theory of truth.

Consideration of the subject of logic may help to clarify matters. Dewey's basic claim here is that logical forms arise within inquiry, with a warranted assertion as the result desired. He also maintains, however, that this inquiry "must itself satisfy logical requirements."[42] That this reasoning is circular does not escape Dewey; his answer, John E. Smith observes, takes the form of a claim that inquiry itself develops, over time, standards for future inquiry. Smith continues, "This answer, it is clear, presupposes the all-important fact—the basis of Dewey's entire position—of science as a 'self-corrective process' which presumably operates successfully without appeal to 'standards *ab extra.*' "[43] The only word I would change in Smith's statement is "fact." The term "faith" seems much more in order, especially since the word "presumably" is in the same sentence.

I have covered much ground, but we should now be in a position to trace Dewey's defense of democratic politics more precisely. Democratic political institutions are justified because the broader democratic ideal is justified. That ideal in turn depends on Dewey's two sorts of "faith in human nature": one individualistic, the other collectivistic.

First, there is the independent strand of thought that democratic political institutions "rest back upon the idea that no man or limited set of men is wise enough or good enough to rule others without their consent." Here Dewey seems to be looking at individuals in isolation from one another and from the environment long enough to determine that no one person can contribute so much more than others to our transactions with the environment that he or she is entitled to political authority over them. This individualistic faith in human nature is not necessarily implied by the collectivistic sort; for Dewey admits that people have significant native differences from one another. Thus, because Dewey concedes on occasion that the majority of people have not fulfilled their potential, it makes sense to call this individualistic sort a "faith."

The second, collectivistic sense might be better called Dewey's faith in a "situation," in the transactions between human being and environment. We are well situated in our surroundings, Dewey believes, in that not only can we "get by" in the world from day to day, but we can also derive meaning from our relations with it. Because Dewey has no doubt about the existence of a world that operates independently of human purposes, a world that often frustrates those purposes, this faith in the situations of humans necessitates faith that the experimental method deals adequately with the world.[44] Thus for Dewey democracy as a way of life depends crucially on a faith in scientific method; that is not to say, however, that the scientific method is our only means of experiencing what is real.

This second sort of faith in human nature appears to be more momentous in Dewey's democratic thought; for one way to state his justification of democracy is that democratic society and government allow for the greatest growth of meaning, for the most meaningful human lives. It is meaning, according to Dewey, that separates human life from other animal life: "it is the agency for elevating man into the realm of what is usually called the ideal and spiritual" (*EN,* 7). The creation of meaning is an interpersonal affair, no more purely subjective than are morals. "Meaning is not indeed a psychic existence; it is primarily a property of behavior" involving two or more persons—behavior that Dewey calls "cooperative," although the interaction may or may not be amiable (*EN,* 141). It makes sense, then, that forms of society and government be evaluated according to how they promote the quality that makes our lives human.

Meaning is possible only through language and communication. Language is perhaps the leading "tool" that provides the natural link between the physical and the ideal. That it is a natural link, however, does not mean that it can be fully explained: "Of all affairs, communication is the most wonderful. . . . [T]hat the fruit of communication should be participation, sharing, is a wonder by the side of which transubstantiation pales. . . . Events turn into objects, things with a meaning" (*EN,* 132). To let our wonder make us resort to a nonnatural explanation for communication, though, is to establish a purposeless gap between physical existences on the one hand and meanings, reified into "essences," on the other hand (*EN,* 133).

Continuity expresses the lack of that gap; here we may at least begin to see the relation between the earlier account of continuity and Dewey's faith in the human situation.[45] The ability of two human beings to make connections through language presupposes that there is no existential gap between them. In other words, it presupposes continuity in the sense of continuum among organisms and environment. From this point, it appears that continuity—in the sense of continuum at least—is the starting point for Dewey's justification of democracy, because it is the assumption behind his faith in the human situation.

Yet the matter is more complicated, for we must realize that for Dewey the relation between communication and continuity works the other way as well. Just as communication depends on a prior continuum, so communication also promotes continuity in the sense of growth or development. Communication can help to dissolve discontinuities and enable the members of a community to solve problems cooperatively. Thus continuity is of direct, practical significance for Dewey's democratic theory. Of course, this is not to say that communication will always be fruitful; it may instead aggravate discontinuities among people and make further communication more difficult. But when we recognize the dependence of continuity as growth upon communication, we see that the principle of continuity is not simply the starting point for the justification of democracy.

Recall Dewey's claim that the "ultimate sanction" of democracy is that it "releases and relieves" human nature. The release and relief come through the opportunity to create and express meanings in life. The justification of democracy is that it, more than any other form of society and government, allows for the creation and expression of meanings, because it offers the greatest opportunity for all members of a sociopolitical community to develop their potential.

Yet Dewey realizes that he must ask whether democracy has support beyond the human ideal of creation of meaning, more so than other forms of society and government. If it does not, how can it be worth our devotion? Is democracy an idle dream, or will the world support our democratic efforts? In an article entitled "Philosophy and Democracy" he gives a sketch of the kind of metaphysics required for the existence of democracy. He first criticizes two alternative metaphysics. The first of those is "a metaphysics of feudalism," which "has thought of things in the world as occupying certain grades of value, or as having fixed degrees of truth, ranks of reality."[46] That metaphysics has been used to justify many varieties of political and social inequality from the ancient Greeks onwards. But it is not only ancient and medieval authorities who have opposed a truly democratic metaphysics; the same can be said for the liberal tradition of "atomistic individualism," which "makes equality quantitative, and hence individuality something external and mechanical rather than qualitative and unique."[47] Dewey insists that in "social and moral matters, equality does not mean mathematical equivalence. . . . It means that no matter how great the quantitative differences of ability, strength, position, wealth, such differences are negligible in comparison with something else—the fact of individuality, the manifestation of something irreplaceable. . . . It implies, so to speak, a metaphysical mathematics of the incommensurable in which each speaks for itself and demands consideration on its own behalf."[48] In short, Dewey's claim is that equality implies individuality, or *is* individuality.

Individuality may take a destructive course, however, for it "tends to isolation and independence." Thus individuality needs as a complement "fraternity," or "association and interaction without limit." Dewey refers to this association and interaction as "continuity," apparently intending the sense of growth (or at least the opportunity for growth). Continuity in the sense of continuum seems to be implied too, since Dewey objects to the social contract "idea of a natural individual in his isolation possessed of full-fledged wants" (*PIP*, 299).

It is this metaphysics—the description of "a universe in which there is real uncertainty and contingency, a world which is not all in, and never will be, a world which in some respect is incomplete and in the making"—that offers a home to democratic aspirations.[49] This account of nature, including the notion of continuity, is, if anything, what gives "an encouraging nod" to our democratic efforts.[50] That "nod" seems to be some sort of justification of democracy. If I read Dewey correctly, he is not claiming that such a metaphysics guarantees the success of democratic society and government, only that it warrants the attempt.

We have not yet traced, however, the arguments that he gives for the principle of continuity. How does he arrive at that principle? It is difficult or impossible to say with certainty. Let us first look at continuity as a metaphysical conclusion. Now what exactly are the grounds of Dewey's metaphysics? Here one who attempts to trace the links in the chain of Dewey's philosophical views yet remain faithful to Dewey's intentions is puzzled. The goal of metaphysics is "detection and description of the generic traits of existence" (*EN*, 52). Only two years after publication of *Experience and Nature* Dewey says of his method in that book that it "differs no whit from that of any investigator who, by making certain observations and experiments, and by utilizing the existing body of ideas available for calculation and interpretation, concludes that he really succeeds in finding out something about some limited aspect of nature."[51] As numerous scholars have noted, it is almost completely unclear how Dewey accomplishes this task through application of empirical method. What are we then to say? The possibilities seem to be two: either go along with Dewey and attribute his metaphysics to confidence in empiricism as the method of successful inquiry, or attribute it to some sort of intuition. The former option is problematic but is certainly in keeping with the commonly received view that Dewey's philosophy rises or falls with the merits of his claims about science.[52]

My inclination toward the former option is strengthened upon examining Dewey's writing on continuity as a presupposition. Around the time of writing his major work on metaphysics, Dewey appears to identify the notion of continuity as a presupposition in his thought: "A denial of the separation [of natural and social] is not only possible to a sane mind, but is demanded by any methodological adoption of the principle of continuity . . .—if that is to be termed a hypothesis which cannot be denied without self-contradiction."[53] Unfortunately, Dewey does not explain why the principle of continuity cannot be denied without self-contradiction. How is it true that one cannot deny the continuity of, in this case, natural and social without invoking it?

Fortunately, the preceding is not all that Dewey says on the matter. In *Democracy and Education* he contrasts his theory of knowing to others by averring that his theory assumes the notion of continuity (*DE*, 343). Other theories, he claims, tend to dichotomize empirical versus rational knowing, learning as storehouse of material versus learning as doing, passivity versus activity, emotions versus intellect, theory versus practice. He then presents two main arguments for continuity—in this context, of mind and body. First, progress in physiology and psychology has demonstrated the connections among the mind, the nervous system, and the body. The "nervous system is only a specialized mechanism for keeping all bodily activities working together. . . . While each motor response [to a stimulus] is adjusted to the state of affairs indicated through the sense–organs, that motor response shapes the next sensory stimulus" (*DE*, 346). Dewey here implicitly draws upon his own early, seminal article "The Reflex Arc Concept in Psychology" (1896).[54]

Second, the discovery of biological evolution teaches the continuity of complex forms of life from simpler forms. "As activity becomes more complex, coordinating a greater number of factors in space and time, intelligence plays a more and more marked role, for it has a larger span of the future to forecast and plan for. The effect upon the theory of knowing is to displace the notion that it is the activity of a mere on-looker or spectator of the world, the notion which goes with the idea of knowing as something complete in itself" (*DE*, 347). Here Dewey evidently combines the senses of continuity as continuum and growth. He repeats this latter argument six years later, in *Human Nature and Conduct*, where he writes, "Continuity of growth [from one habit to another] not atomism [of habits] is . . . the alternative to fixity of principles and aims" (*HNC*, 168). Moral principles and aims develop over time; in effect, this continuity is implied in accepting the teaching of evolution (or at least in not accepting some sort of supernaturalism).

Because Dewey presents these arguments for his notion of continuity instead of taking it as an assumption, I do not think we may say that there is a clear final point for his defense of democracy. I do not think we may say that the ultimate point is his principle of continuity, for the growth or development that partially constitutes continuity depends on communication. I do not think we may say that the ultimate point is his account of communication, for communication depends on existence of a continuum among organisms and environment. It is an odd defense of democracy, it seems to me, more foundational than antifoundational, but not traditionally foundational. The political theory does depend on the metaphysics: Dewey clearly believes that if his principle of continuity were conclusively refuted, the traditional problems of philosophy would recur. How the mind can know the world would become once again a question in need of an answer. If knowledge were problematic, then Dewey's faith in the human situation, the transactions between organism and environment, would be problematic also. This confidence, we have seen, underlies his conviction concerning the broad democratic ideal, which in turn underlies his advocacy of democratic political institutions. Yet the relation between political theory and metaphysics is reciprocal: continuity depends on communication as well.

If metaphysical dualisms were conclusively established, would Dewey remain a democrat? Here one can only speculate. If an all-encompassing unity, an Absolute, were needed to bring together what is found to be separate, then Dewey's criticism of the Absolute would apply: as one scholar summarizes it, the Absolute renders "human action unnecessary and doomed to incompletion, forever straining toward and never capable of attaining the self-certainty of the Absolute as it is in and for itself."[55] If it is an Absolute that determines the meaning of human existence, then what is left for humans to do? Dewey might then find democracy preferable to other forms of government for certain reasons; but democracy would be merely a form of government, not a way of life.

DEWEY'S INTERPRETERS REEXAMINED

The view of Dewey I have advanced is in stark contrast to Rorty's claim that Dewey is not concerned with "providing theoretical foundations for practice."[56] It is true that Dewey wants to "free us up for practice," in the sense that he wants to turn philosophers' attention away from what he considers artificial, abstract problems and toward real problems arising from life as it is lived. Dewey would object, though, that "practice" cannot be so neatly treated in terms of distinct spheres, such as the "political," as Rorty thinks.

Dewey's political theory is far removed from Rorty's. One of the few similarities to note is that, like Rorty, Dewey draws a distinction between public and private concerns. Yet not only does Dewey assert that democracy is fully realized only when it affects conduct in all areas, including what is properly private, he makes an even stronger statement: As to political democracy, "experience has proved that it cannot stand in isolation. It can be effectively maintained only where democracy is social," where it is "moral."[57] The sort of fragmentation of public and private conduct that Rorty sanctions is found infeasible by Dewey. Undemocratic habits in the private realm will ultimately undermine democratic habits in the public sphere. While, to the best of my knowledge, Dewey does not offer an opinion as to what is acceptable public discourse, the tenor of his position is that controversial opinions, such as religious beliefs, should be brought into the open as fully as possible to receive intelligent scrutiny.[58]

Against Rorty, I contend that the fact that Dewey is as concerned as he is with the justification of democracy makes his thought more, not less, worthy of serious consideration. But I differ here also from Sidney Hook, who says that Dewey is not sufficiently concerned with the question of justification. Hook was probably Dewey's most prominent student and one of his leading interpreters, so his thoughts are worth quoting at length:

> "How numerous and varied are the interests which are commonly [*sic*] shared? How full and free is the interplay with other forms of association?" Using these as moral criteria, the superiority of the democratic community to all other forms of communal association is easy to establish.
>
> Actually this derivation of the validity of democratic society is circular, and some may even claim it is question-begging because the very choice of criteria presupposes an ideal family. In a series of later writings, especially his *The Public and Its Problems, Liberalism and Social Action,* and *Freedom and Culture,* Dewey returns to the question of the

justification of democracy. . . . It is a warranted surmise that had *De-mocracy and Education* been written after the rise of totalitarianism and its challenge to the democratic faith, Dewey would have devoted more pages to the problem of justification.[59]

If Hook were correct that Dewey intended the two questions quoted above from *Democracy and Education* to serve by themselves as justification of democratic government, then Dewey's defense certainly would be circular and begging the question. At the beginning of the paragraph in which those two questions occur, Dewey does speak of "the need of a measure for the worth of any given mode of social life" (*DE*, 88). As I have attempted to show in this chapter, however, he does not treat the worth of the moral (i.e., beyond political) democratic ideal as self-evident. The worth of the moral ideal is tied to a metaphysical view.

Hook is correct in saying that Dewey deals with the problem of justification in the three books mentioned above; but in none of the three does Dewey give what may be taken to be his fullest solution, for in none does he devote real attention to continuity. In *The Public and Its Problems* he writes that democracy represents a choice of the most good with the least evil; as to what is good, he says that the democratic ideal "consists in having a responsible share according to capacity in forming and directing the activities of the groups to which one belongs and in participating according to need in the values which the groups sustain" (*PIP*, 327–28). In *Liberalism and Social Action* he makes a brief remark that the purpose of liberal government is development of the capacities of all individuals, but he says no more about justification.[60]

The fullest treatment among the books cited by Hook is found in *Freedom and Culture*, in a chapter entitled "Democracy and America," where Dewey stresses the need "to face the issue of the moral ground of political institutions" (*FC*, 179). The need is particularly great, he asserts, since belief in natural law or natural rights is no longer credible. It must be replaced with "a faith based on ideas that are now intellectually credible and that are consonant with present economic conditions." What is required is "an adequate theory of human nature in its relations to democracy" (*FC*, 150). Dewey does not provide the theory there, however; he stops by calling for "faith in the potentialities of human nature," where "the word *faith* is intentionally used" to substitute for a supposedly discredited Christianity, formerly thought to be a grounding for democracy (*FC,* 151, 152). As I have attempted to demonstrate, this faith is linked to his belief in the principle of continuity.

In arguing for this relation of Dewey's metaphysics to his political theory, I disagree somewhat with the interpretation of R. W. Sleeper. Sleeper alleges that Dewey did not intend his notion of continuity "to function as a foundation on which to build a system. It is clear that Dewey views continuity as merely a feature of specific situations and circumstances, a feature that certain other situations and circumstances lack."[61] In the context from which I quote, Sleeper is discussing realism and idealism, so by "system" he apparently means metaphysics; but by implication I think his words would apply to a system of political theory as well. But Sleeper's claim overgeneralizes. While continuity may be lacking in certain situations—that is, certain things are discrete instead of overtly connected to one another—continuity in the sense of existential continuum between organism and environment is never lacking in any situation, according to Dewey. Sleeper continues, "If anything should be regarded as Dewey's first philosophy, it is his genetic account of communication."[62] I would argue instead that for Dewey communication is impossible without the principle of continuity in the sense of continuum between organism and environment. Sleeper would be correct, however, to argue for the dependence of continuity as growth on communication.

In a remarkable article written in 1939, Dewey appears to make his peace with foundationalist philosophy. He retracts remarks made in previous works in which he disparaged philosophical system. He claims that "any theory of activity in social and moral matters, liberal or otherwise, which is not grounded in a comprehensive philosophy seems to me to be only a projection of arbitrary personal preference."[63] In other words, any valid political theory must be based on a philosophy that deals with metaphysical and epistemological matters.

Yet it has been alleged by those who see Dewey as clearly in the antifoundationalist camp that his thought took an antimetaphysical turn late in his life. One scholar, T. Z. Lavine, claims that Dewey and Arthur Bentley, Dewey's coauthor in his last book, engaged in a "rejection of metaphysics."[64] As grounds for her position she may have had in mind Dewey's comment that their work should not be read as a "rival metaphysical scheme."[65]

Lavine is incorrect, however, if she implies that *Knowing and the*

Known implies a rejection of Dewey's teaching in *Experience and Nature*.[66] As she herself observes, the central purpose of *Knowing and the Known* (aside from criticism of formal logic and logical positivism) was to construct a set of terms, free from vagueness and the dualistic connotations of traditional philosophy, that would be useful for inquiry into human behavior. In the process of collaboration with Bentley, Dewey agreed with him that certain terms he had used in past works did not pass muster; and indeed, these terms include "experience," central to Dewey's metaphysics. Yet the basis on which judgment is delivered implies the core of *Experience and Nature*: it is "transactional," in contrast to "self-actional" and "interactional." Dewey and Bentley define these bases or modes as follows:

> *Self-action:* where things are viewed as acting under their own powers. *Inter-action:* where [existentially separate] thing is balanced against [existentially separate] thing in causal interconnection. *Trans-action:* where systems of description and naming are employed to deal with aspects and phases of action, without final attribution to "elements" or other presumptively detachable or independent "entities," "essences," or "realities," and without isolation of presumptively detachable "relations" from such detachable "elements."[67]

Against Lavine, who claims that Dewey and Bentley are engaged in "denying cognitive significance to metaphysics," I contend that this transactional mode confirms, not renounces, the principle of continuity, so clearly involved in Dewey's metaphysics.[68] Although the terms may change (at one point Dewey pledges in correspondence to Bentley to avoid the word "organism" because of its signification of existential discontinuity), the transactional formulation implies something very much like continuity in the sense of continuum, if not also growth, in its reaction against the interactional formulation.

Moreover, in the same year in which *Knowing and the Known* was published, Dewey makes the following statement:

> I now realize that it was exceedingly naive of me to suppose that it was possible to rescue the word [i.e., "metaphysics"] from its deeply engrained traditional use. I derive what consolation may be possible from promising myself never to use the words again in connection with any aspect of any part of my own position. . . . And while I think

the *words* used were most unfortunate I still believe that that which they were used to name is genuine and important.[69]

In the same article Dewey rejects use of the word "metaphysical" "in the sense it bears in the classic tradition based on Aristotle."[70] As the last sentence of the quotation makes perfectly clear, though, he does not renounce the substance of *Experience and Nature*. In an unpublished article probably completed in 1950, Dewey summarizes his work with Bentley as follows: "The basic postulates of the view presented are (1) that knowing, as inquiry, is [a] way or distinctive form of behavior, and (2) that like all forms of behavior [it] is *transactional* in pattern in that it is constituted by the cooperation or *working together* of activities which, *when they are distinguished,* are referred respectively to an organism in one respect and to environing conditions in another regard."[71] This summary combines the "transactional" approach of *Knowing and the Known* with the emphasis on functional, not existential, discontinuities (e.g., between organism and environment) of *Experience and Nature*. It is clear, then, that Dewey does not see the two works as basically incompatible.

CRITICISM OF DEWEY'S METAPHYSICAL APPROACH TO DEMOCRACY

The preceding discussion should show that I find it misleading to call Dewey a nonfoundationalist or antifoundationalist. He does not seek to avoid a self-refuting relativism through fantasizing or romanticism. I have my doubts about how well he does so, as I shall explain in chapter 5. Continuity is crucial in his metaphysics, and it operates as a basis for his political theory. Of course, we must remember that his work is an attack on all previous philosophers who have, in one way or another, tried to find or build a philosophical foundation for politics.

While not disagreeing with the view that Dewey provides a metaphysical justification of politics, David Steiner says that "Dewey's justification for democratic politics, and for the education on which those politics depend, is found in his theory of knowledge. To put a complex matter simply, Dewey believes that of all political systems a certain form of democracy best realizes the capacity of life to embody 'meaning.' "[72] Hilary Putnam agrees: Dewey provides an "*epistemological justification of democracy.*"⁷³ Democracy is "the precondition for the full application of intelligence to the solution of social problems." Both Steiner and Putnam mean that the conditions for the fullest pursuit of knowledge require democracy. Unlike Rorty, neither Putnam nor Steiner thinks less of Dewey for being concerned with metaphysical questions. Both of them see the lack of thoughtfulness in Rorty's conventionalist approach to political democracy. That insight leads both of them to support, in one way or another, Dewey's metaphysics (Steiner) or pragmatism in general (Putnam).

Only the sort of dogmatist who refuses to think about ultimate questions, because he is convinced that the human mind is incapable of solving them, would blame Dewey for being concerned with metaphysical questions. If we are not so quick to accept the postmodern creed, then we realize that Dewey should not be blamed for that concern. The Dewey who wrote *Experience and Nature* does not present a fully clear "naturalistic metaphysics," to be sure, but it is understandable that he focuses his attention on identifying "generic traits"—universal descriptions of existences; he sees the radical instability of our answers to more particular questions concerning such things as forms of government until we have arrived at adequate answers to more ultimate questions.

Nor should we blame Dewey for refusing to swear off talk of "truth," "nature," or other terms associated with foundationalist positions. Dewey is not the first philosopher to aspire to transcend traditional philosophical problems who has relied on traditional terms: Nietzsche's use of "truth," sometimes in quotation marks and sometimes not, and his continued reliance on "nature," often in quotation marks, illustrate this.⁷⁴ Dewey's attempt to find "warranted assertions" (if not universal truth) in the form of generic traits of existence represents a sharp rejection of Rorty's willingness to understand truth within the bounds of communities.⁷⁵ To answer a question raised in the first chapter, that rejection draws him closer to Jefferson's reliance on "Laws of Nature and of Nature's God" than to Rorty's appeal to communities; yet Dewey's denial of universal truth seems to put him closer to Rorty than to Jefferson.⁷⁶

Dewey's effort is more worthy of appreciation upon realization that at the time Dewey was writing his metaphysics, logical positivism was beginning to exert an influence on Anglo-American philosophy. We must note his refusal to join the logical positivists in their embrace of the dichotomy between fact and value, or the derivative analytic philosophers in their plan to make philosophy "scientific" by reducing it to problems of linguistic analysis—even if *Knowing and the Known* is guilty of partaking of the spirit of logical positivism in its belief that solving philosophical problems requires first rewriting the philosophical dictionary. I believe that the book is guilty of this. Dewey's claim that moral and political philosophy must be "grounded in a comprehensive philosophy" demonstrates his general sympathy with those who would make philosophy systematic. But he knows that the approach of analytic philosophy had sufficient difficulty dealing with Nietzsche's perspectivist attack that he cannot endorse it. He knows, in short, that modern science needs some explanation for itself, and he at least begins to understand that a transcending of traditional philosophical problems would require such an explanation.

What we may ask is whether Dewey finds the right way to begin to transcend traditional philosophical problems. Are we wise to accept his principle of continuity? If the claim is that continuity, in the sense of some sort of connection between organism and environment, is an inherent aspect of human sensibility, that is hard to deny. That there is some relation, and not total rupture, between human being and environment appears to be a legitimate inference from the human abilities to make sense of the environment and to have coherent lives. But the claim for an existential continuum, as a metaphysical point, is a different matter; it does not follow that we may draw any conclusions about metaphysical relations from the relation between human and environment. A full metaphysical account, if we had it, might reveal a separation between organism and environment more pronounced than whatever connection there is.

It might also be argued that continuity in the sense of continuum is a scientifically proven tenet: human beings evolved from their environment and therefore must be considered as ontologically connected to their surroundings (instead of as the creation of divine intervention in the environment). One need not deny the central principle of evolutionary science in order to think it would be rash to draw a metaphysical conclusion—even pertaining to a naturalistic metaphysics—from evolutionary science. As Sidney Hook admits, Dewey's "assertion that these [generic] traits and qualities that mark the human condition are the mark of nature, too" goes unproven.[77] Yet Hook accepts some notion of continuity, remarking that it is "fortified by the cumulative results of the natural, biological-medical, and cultural disciplines" and that it explains how thought can affect the world.[78]

This qualified assent to Dewey's notion of continuity seems to me to strike the correct balance. Hook reasonably criticizes Dewey's metaphysics for being too abstract and thus preventing full agreement, but he cannot entirely reject continuity.[79] I would say that we do not even need the "natural, biological-medical, and cultural disciplines" to accept some sort of continuity; human experience is sufficient.

Hook, however, seems also to be referring to continuity in the second sense mentioned earlier, that of growth. This is the sense that appears to dominate in Dewey's *Logic*. Dewey's purpose in that book is to describe a theory of human inquiry that fulfills the requirements of modern science and illustrates the development of rational thought from "lower" biological operations. Yet, as Ernest Nagel claims, "[I]t is not at all clear that the stipulated continuity between the logical and the biological is either a necessary or a sufficient condition that an otherwise sound account of modern scientific method must satisfy."[80] To make a metaphysical claim that higher organisms or operations always grow out of lower ones is to make a questionable assertion.

In sum, the notion of continuity seems to me both indisputable, in one sense, and highly questionable, in another. As a presupposition of Dewey's metaphysics—or of any human experience—continuity is inescapable: there must be some connection between organism and environment. As a metaphysical conclusion concerning growth, continuity is the result, according to Dewey, of application of scientific method. In that case, continuity is verified by scientific method; but scientific method itself, according to Dewey, cannot be explained without reference to continuity in the sense of continuum. Thus Dewey, in some sense, presupposes what he sets out to prove.

To question the principle of continuity is not necessarily to affirm the metaphysical dualisms (subject/object, individual/community) that Dewey uses it to attack. In a review of Alan Ryan's book, Stephen Holmes has asked "if there is really no rational ground for retaining some of the dualisms that Dewey tried to flatten out or dismantle."[81] Holmes does not make clear what sort of dualisms he might wish to retain or what it would mean to do so. Why would we want to retain metaphysical dualisms, however, without sufficient basis for doing so?

Dewey's claim that any moral or political philosophy that "is not grounded in a comprehensive philosophy" is merely "a projection of arbitrary personal preference" clearly marks him as offering a more thoughtful approach than Rorty. But is that claim correct? That is a difficult question. If it is correct, then we must solve the ultimate questions (those crucial for attaining "a comprehensive philosophy"), such as, "Is there a God who cares for human beings?" before we can solve the proximate ones, such as "What is the best form of government?" At least, according to Dewey, if we cannot solve the ultimate questions, then we cannot legitimately regard our solutions to the proximate ones as having any validity. We shall return to this question in the last chapter.

But first, a solution to that difficult question requires at least that we understand arguably the most important aspect of Dewey's "comprehensive philosophy": his aesthetics, which is crucial to his account of the kind of "experience" democracy should foster. In particular, although we have not noted it here, the next chapter will detail the relation of scientific method to artistic method and to aesthetics in general, and the implications that his aesthetics has for his political thought, especially for his reflections on civic education.

NOTES

1. The difficulty of discussing the question of Dewey and foundationalism, or of foundationalism generally, is illustrated by the differing characterizations of Dewey in a series of articles in William J. Gavin, ed., *Context over Foundation: Dewey and Marx,* Sovietica Series, vol. 52 (Dordrecht, Holland: D. Reidel, 1988). Vincent Michael Colapietro says that Dewey and Marx "were instrumental in effecting the transition from foundationalism to contextualism, that is, the transition from the perspective that inquiry necessarily rests upon an ultimate and immutable foundation to the viewpoint that investigation always occurs within a provisional and contingent context"; yet "neither is entirely free from all forms of foundationalism—at least from the perspective of the other" ("From 'Individual' to 'Subject': Marx and Dewey on the Person," 12). According to Colapietro, Dewey's faith in rational persuasion, in the power of the democratic ideal, grounds his specific political proposals: "Indeed, this faith is as fixed and final for Dewey as, say, the *cogito* is for Descartes (to select one outstanding example of the foundationalist thesis)" (ibid., 13). William J. Gavin asserts that "Dewey is clearly an anti-foundationalist philosopher," where "anti-founda-

tionalist" seems to mean contextualist, adhering to the view that human thought can be true not timelessly but only in relation to a context ("Text, Context, and the Existential Limit: A Jamesian Strain in Marx and Dewey," 50). Garry M. Brodsky identifies Dewey as a "non-foundationalist" ("Politics, Culture and Society in Marx and Dewey," 77). Because of "its frequent self-conscious appeals to clearly identified empirical and fallible scientific conclusions and its critical character, Dewey's philosophy does not easily lend itself to being construed as foundationalist" (ibid., 79). Dewey's metaphysics "does not lend itself to de-contextualist, foundationalist purposes. . . . [T]he features he emphasizes are the ones we should expect to find emphasized by a contextualist" (ibid., 82). Peter T. Manicas claims that "Dewey's was a politics that needed no foundations" ("Philosophy and Politics: A Historical Approach to Marx and Dewey," 170). Alfonso J. Damico writes, "Whether conceptualized as a 'conversation,' (Richard Rorty), as 'inquiry' (Dewey), or in terms of a 'movement' (Marx), it is practice itself, not epistemology and axiology, that privileges one or another account of political life" ("The Politics After Deconstruction: Rorty, Dewey, and Marx," 179). According to Damico, Dewey is "non-foundational"; Rorty, "anti-foundational." None of these articles takes sufficient notice of the idea of continuity in Dewey's thought, which I explore in this chapter.

2. Richard Rorty, "Thugs and Theorists: A Reply to Bernstein," *Political Theory* 15 (November 1987): 577.

3. Richard J. Bernstein, "One Step Forward, Two Steps Backward: Richard Rorty on Liberal Democracy and Philosophy," *Political Theory* 15 (November 1987): 560.

4. John Dewey, *The Quest for Certainty* (1929), in L4 (1984): 206. Hereafter I shall refer to this work parenthetically in the text as QC followed by page number.

5. John Stuart Mill, *Utilitarianism,* edited by George Sher (Indianapolis: Hackett, 1979 [1861]), 34; John Dewey and James H. Tufts, *Ethics,* rev. ed. (1932), in L7:192. The first edition of Dewey and Tufts's *Ethics* was published in 1908. Since we know that Dewey wrote the part of the 1908 edition corresponding to the part in the revised edition from which this quotation is taken, it seems reasonable to surmise that he, not Tufts, wrote this passage.

6. John Dewey, contributions to *A Cyclopedia of Education* (volumes 3–5) (1912–13), in M7 (1979): 363.

7. John Dewey, *The Ethics of Democracy* (1888), in E1 (1975): 240.

8. John Dewey and James H. Tufts, *Ethics* (1908), in M5 (1983): 424.

9. John Dewey, "The Need of an Industrial Education in an Industrial Democracy" (1916), in M10 (1980): 138.

10. John Patrick Diggins appears to be very unfamiliar with Dewey's educational thought when he writes, "Dewey's philosophy allows laissez-faire in edu-

cational and moral life that it denies in political life. Seeing the economy as haphazard, he saw schooling as spontaneous. Thus in the schoolroom Dewey advocated hands off, a decidedly noninterventionist philosophy that would impose no system or structure upon the process of learning." Diggins, *Promise of Pragmatism,* 305.

11. John Dewey, *Reconstruction in Philosophy* (1920), in M12 (1982): 186. Hereafter I shall refer to this work parenthetically in the text as *RP* followed by page number.

12. For criticism of Marxism see *FC,* 124–30.

13. Dewey, "Need of an Industrial Education," 137–38.

14. John Dewey, "Democracy and Educational Administration" (1937), in L11:217, 218.

15. Robert Horwitz, "John Dewey," in *History of Political Philosophy,* ed. Strauss and Cropsey, 858.

16. John Dewey, "What Are We Fighting For?" (1918), in M11:106.

17. Dewey, "Democracy and Educational Administration," 218.

18. Ibid., 219.

19. John Dewey, "Human Nature" (1932), in L6 (1985): 31.

20. Dewey, "Does Human Nature Change?" 286.

21. Ibid., 287.

22. John Dewey, "What Are States of Mind?" (1912), in M7:36, 38.

23. John Dewey, *Experience and Nature,* 2d ed. (1929), in L1:10. The first edition was published in 1925. Hereafter I shall refer to this work parenthetically in the text as *EN* followed by page number.

24. My understanding of Dewey's notion of continuity has benefited from correspondence by electronic mail on the John Dewey discussion list with Thomas Alexander, Randy Auxier, Craig Cunningham, David Hildebrand, and Bill Myers.

25. For a thorough account of the development of pragmatism see Thayer, *Meaning and Action.*

26. S. Morris Eames, *Pragmatic Naturalism: An Introduction* (Carbondale: Southern Illinois University Press, 1977), 25.

27. John Dewey, "The Need for a Recovery of Philosophy" (1917), in M10:12.

28. John Dewey, "Experience, Knowledge and Value: A Rejoinder" (1939), in L14:30.

29. Hilary Putnam neglects this fact when he claims that Dewey's underlying premises are "some very 'ordinary' assumptions": "to acknowledge the language, the community, and the world as one, in all their entanglement with one another." Dewey never says that organism and environment are "one"—a claim that would be neither ordinary nor clear if Dewey should make it. Putnam,

"Reconsideration of Deweyan Democracy," 226. In effect, Putnam cedes too much to Rorty's interpretation of Dewey when, in a section of that essay entitled "Dewey's Metaphysics (or Lack Thereof)," he regards Dewey's metaphysics as "a concession to the philosophical style of his (and our) contemporaries."

30. Dewey, *Logic,* 26, 30. Raymond Boisvert seems to link together continuity in the sense of continuum and continuity in the sense of growth by referring to both "the *continuity* of humans and the natural world" and "biological continuity" as one notion. Raymond D. Boisvert, *Dewey's Metaphysics* (New York: Fordham University Press, 1988), 68, 69.

31. Craig A. Cunningham makes this distinction in a message on the John Dewey discussion list (dewey-l@postoffice.cso.uiuc.edu, "continuity [and discontinuity]," 15 September 1995).

32. Thomas M. Alexander, *John Dewey's Theory of Art, Experience, and Nature: The Horizons of Feeling* (Albany: State University of New York Press, 1987), 99.

33. Thayer, *Meaning and Action,* 464n14.

34. Here I agree with the conclusion of Alexander, *Dewey's Theory,* 103. I disagree with Thayer, who writes, "If it [i.e., continuity] holds in any case, if it is always true, it in fact tells us nothing." Thayer, *Meaning and Action,* 465. If continuity as continuum is present in any case, it may explain to us a precondition for continuity as growth.

35. See John Dewey, "The Development of American Pragmatism" (1925), in L2:13.

36. John Dewey, "The Problem of Truth" (1911), in M6 (1978): 19–20. This account necessarily simplifies Dewey's view of truth. R. W. Sleeper maintains that Dewey rejects the typical pragmatic theory that a claim is true if we find its consequences satisfactory. See R. W. Sleeper, *The Necessity of Pragmatism: John Dewey's Conception of Philosophy* (New Haven, Conn.: Yale University Press, 1986), 140–41.

37. John Dewey, "Logical Conditions of a Scientific Treatment of Morality" (1903), in M3 (1977): 8.

38. Ibid., 15.

39. Dewey, contributions to *A Cyclopedia of Education* (vols. 3–5), 364.

40. Dewey, *Logic,* 15.

41. Dewey, "The Problem of Truth," 22.

42. Dewey, *Logic,* 13.

43. Smith, *Purpose and Thought,* 99.

44. On the frustration of human purposes see Dewey, "Need for Recovery of Philosophy," 18.

45. I am grateful to an anonymous reviewer for comments on communication and continuity.

46. John Dewey, "Philosophy and Democracy" (1919), in M11:51.

47. Ibid., 52–53.

48. Ibid., 53.

49. Ibid., 50.

50. Ibid., 48.

51. John Dewey, "'Half-Hearted Naturalism'" (1927), in L3:76. In the same year Dewey writes to a frequent correspondent that he has tried to "break down" such "barriers" as those between "man and the world" "by showing that facts show there are no such separations." John Dewey to Scudder Klyce, 21 October 1927, Scudder Klyce Papers, General Correspondence: John Dewey: Manuscript Division, Library of Congress, Washington, D.C.; quoted in Rockefeller, *John Dewey*, 492–93.

52. Dewey adds to the mystery of the derivation of the generic traits of existence by claiming that "the most adequate definition of the basic traits of natural existence can be had only when its properties are most fully displayed—a condition which is met in the degree of the scope and intimacy of the interactions realized" (*EN*, 201). As we shall see in the next chapter, the highest degree of scope and intimacy is found in aesthetic experience. Thus Dewey appears to be holding aesthetic experience as a prerequisite of any application of scientific method that has as its goal the detection of the generic traits of existence. Thomas Alexander cautions, however, that "Dewey would not go so far as to say that art reveals the *truth* of nature." Alexander, *Dewey's Theory*, 102. Aesthetic experience is rather a precondition of using science to arrive at the truth.

53. John Dewey, "The Inclusive Philosophical Idea" (1928), in L3:45.

54. John Dewey, "The Reflex Arc Concept in Psychology" (1896), in E5:96–109.

55. Alexander, *Dewey's Theory*, 43.

56. I am certainly not the first to point out this fact, albeit I try to do so in more detail. See, for example, the following works: Thomas M. Alexander, "Richard Rorty and Dewey's Metaphysics of Experience," *Southwest Philosophical Studies* 5 (1980): 24–35; Bernstein, "One Step Forward," 538–63; Garry Brodsky, "Rorty's Interpretation of Pragmatism," *Transactions of the Charles S. Peirce Society* 18 (1982): 311–37; James Campbell, "Rorty's Use of Dewey," *Southern Journal of Philosophy* 22 (summer 1984): 175–88; Isaac Levi, "Escape from Boredom: Edification According to Rorty," *Canadian Journal of Philosophy* 11 (December 1981): 589–602; Harvey C. Mansfield Jr., "Democracy and the Great Books," *New Republic*, 4 April 1988, 33–37, and "Dewey, All-out Democrat," *Times Literary Supplement*, 24 January 1992, 26; Kai Nielsen, "Scientism, Pragmatism, and the Fate of Philosophy," *Inquiry* 29 (1986): 277–304; R. W. Sleeper, "Rorty's Pragmatism: Afloat in Neurath's Boat, But Why Adrift?" *Transactions of the Charles S. Peirce Society* 21 (1985): 9–20; David Milton Steiner,

"The Possibility of Paideia: Democratic Education in Jean-Jacques Rousseau and John Dewey" (Ph.D. diss., Harvard University, 1989); Westbrook, *Dewey and American Democracy,* 539–42. Rorty is not alone, however, in viewing pragmatist political thinking as divorced from metaphysical considerations: see, for example, Sibyl A. Schwarzenbach, "Rawls, Hegel, and Communitarianism," *Political Theory* 19 (November 1991): 542.

57. Dewey, "Need of an Industrial Education," 138.

58. Rorty continues his misreading of Dewey on the propriety of the introduction of religious beliefs into societal affairs in his "Something to Steer By" (review of Alan Ryan, *John Dewey and the High Tide of American Liberalism*), *London Review of Books,* 20 June 1996, 7–8.

59. Sidney Hook, "Introduction," in M9:xi–xii. Hook, quoting from Dewey's *Democracy and Education,* wrote "commonly" when Dewey wrote "consciously."

60. Dewey, *Liberalism and Social Action,* 25.

61. Sleeper, *Necessity of Pragmatism,* 91. In his book he says that metaphysics is not first philosophy for Dewey. In a later essay, however, he asserts, "For both Dewey and the [American] founders, convictions as to method and procedure in political matters are determined by antecedent considerations of metaphysical perspective." R. W. Sleeper, "John Dewey and the Founding Fathers," in *Values and Value Theory in Twentieth-Century America: Essays in Honor of Elizabeth Flower,* ed. Murray G. Murphey and Ivar Berg (Philadelphia: Temple University Press, 1988), 48.

62. Sleeper, *Necessity of Pragmatism,* 118.

63. Dewey, "Nature in Experience," 150.

64. T. Z. Lavine, "Introduction," in L16 (1989): xxxiii.

65. Dewey and Bentley, *Philosophical Correspondence,* 314.

66. For the claim see Lavine, "Introduction," xxxvii.

67. John Dewey and Arthur F. Bentley, *Knowing and the Known* (1949), in L16:101–2.

68. Lavine, "Introduction," xxxvii.

69. John Dewey, "Experience and Existence: A Comment" (1949), in L16:388.

70. Ibid.

71. Dewey and Bentley, *Philosophical Correspondence,* 657.

72. Steiner, *Rethinking Democratic Education,* 127.

73. Putnam, "Reconsideration of Deweyan Democracy," 217 (italics in original).

74. See Leo Strauss, *Studies in Platonic Political Philosophy* (Chicago: University of Chicago Press, 1983), 189–90.

75. Dewey, *Logic,* 11.

76. Thomas Jefferson, Declaration of Independence, 2d paragraph.

77. Sidney Hook, introduction to L1:x.

78. Ibid., xiii.

79. Ibid., xv.

80. Ernest Nagel, introduction to L12:xv.

81. Stephen Holmes, "Practically Wisdom," *New Republic,* 11 March 1996, 46.

4

DEWEY'S AESTHETICS AND ITS IMPLICATIONS FOR CIVIC EDUCATION

Dewey is in agreement with Friedrich Nietzsche that what human beings become is the result of their powers of creativity. Profoundly antipolitical in one sense, Nietzsche's thought nevertheless has political implications that are, to say the least, not conducive to liberal democracy (whether or not they lead to fascism). Nietzsche rejects any doctrinal claim to human equality that might serve as a basis for democracy.[1] As we have seen, Dewey believes there is so little we can say about human nature that our transactions with one another and with our environment largely determine who we are.[2] Human beings must "create new ideals and values" (*EN*, 4). Yet unlike Nietzsche, Dewey wants to maintain both creativity and democracy. He thus exposes himself to the Nietzschean charge that holding to the former renders the latter a mere personal preference. Those who are friendlier to liberal democracy than Nietzsche is would also ask whether Dewey's emphasis on creativity endangers democracy by opening the door to a political enthusiasm that is the result of an unbridled use of creativity—an enthusiasm that may not respect the requirements of constitutional government.

An emphasis of Dewey's for which he is more famous is his reliance on the modern scientific method as *the* way to arrive at an objective solution to a "problematic situation." Yet Dewey also claims that "science is an art" (*EN*, 268). He sees no inconsistency in encouraging both scientific method and aesthetic experience. In his book on aesthetics that he defends against the charge of inconsistency with his instrumentalism, he asserts as a central tenet that "[k]nowledge is instrumental to the enrichment of immediate experience" (*AE,* 294).

Now Dewey's dictum "Science is an art" might appear to support Rorty's claim that Dewey can properly be considered an intellectual ancestor of postmodern political thought. Rorty has asserted that the postmodern inclination to take a light-minded approach to traditional philosophical problems—in other words, to treat them as reducible to the psychological drives of individuals rather than as conducive to rational argument—"has been an important vehicle of moral progress."[3] On this approach aesthetic considerations such as beauty hold sway in moral matters, because objective, rational considerations, to which they might be subjected, are thought not to be available.[4] But, contrary to Rorty's assertion that Dewey wants the distinction between art and science to be "rubbed out," Dewey does not equate art and science.[5] When he says that "knowledge is instrumental to the enrichment of immediate experience," he believes that rational knowledge is available concerning normative and aesthetic as well as descriptive matters; he rejects the dichotomy of facts and values.

Dewey clearly suggests that creativity and democracy are compatible with each other (*AE,* 345–47). But is his difference from postmodernists such as Rorty concerning the relation between art and science enough to render his coupling of creativity and democracy feasible? In this chapter I shall examine the response that Dewey's thought provides to this potential difficulty and the implications of that response, such as the claim, discussed in chapter 2, that Dewey inadequately discourages tyranny of the majority.

First it will be helpful to identify the central elements of Dewey's teaching on aesthetics and discuss the relation between "immediate experience" and "reflective experience." Then, by comparing and contrasting Dewey with Kant, Burke, Lyotard, and Rorty, I shall offer reasons why we could determine that Dewey's emphasis on creativity would not have consequences deleterious to democracy. But I shall suggest that there are reasons to fear that the centrality of creativity and art for his civic educational reflections would pose a hazard for democracy.

Dewey's teaching on aesthetics is largely found in *Experience and Nature* (published in two editions in 1925 and 1929) and *Art as Experience* (published in 1934). His treatment of the subject is much broader than an analysis of fine art and its effects on the cultured few. Indeed he believes that much misunderstanding of aesthetics and the artistic process has resulted from paying almost exclusive attention to fine art. Thus the source of his teaching is the everyday experiences of most people.

AESTHETICS AND SCIENCE IN DEWEY'S THOUGHT

As we saw in the previous chapter, Dewey claims that experience is not "a veil or screen which shuts us off from nature" (*EN,* 10). Experience for Dewey includes both individual and nature, "organism" and "environment," which, he says, are too often set in existential opposition to each other.

Dewey's definition of art exhibits his opposition to another dichotomy. Throughout *Experience and Nature* he is concerned to refute the notion that there is some sort of activity apart from practical activity that is an end in itself, that a general opposition exists between means and ends in human conduct. He does not deny that this dichotomy is thought to exist by many people and has practical effect. To take two examples, many workers go about their business expecting nothing more fulfilling from their work than that it provide them with subsistence; and many of the same people indulge in amusements seeking only escape from their drudgery. Dewey believes that these attitudes constitute a sad comment on human life, however, and maintains that the ideal activity is found "when the regular, repetitious, and the novel, contingent in nature . . . sustain and inform each other in a productive activity possessed of immanent and directly enjoyed meaning" (*EN,* 271). When an activity is undertaken for its own sake and simultaneously serves another purpose—when it can be said to be both means and end—it is "art."

The first two chapters of *Art as Experience* are concerned with locating the origins of art in everyday experience. Dewey begins with a discussion of the kinds of experiences most people have; the two most important are immediate and reflective.

A person's immediate experience consists of material from the world presented to his or her senses. The person often acts on the basis of this material without thinking, such action leading to further immediate experience. We may *feel* qualities of things in our experience without *thinking* about them. We may also feel qualities of things over time, so that we perceive a flow in events from one stage to another. At some point we may feel that a series of events has reached not just a temporal conclusion, but a consummation—that it has become "*an* experience" (*AE,* 61). Dewey says such an experience has "esthetic quality." When an experience has reached a consummation, when it has become "*an* experience," a certain overall quality is pervasive throughout each of its moments. Dewey calls it the "undefined pervasive quality of an experience . . . which binds together all the defined elements, the objects of which we are focally aware, making them a whole" (*AE,* 198). For Dewey a quality is not something merely internal to an organism but is inherently connected to the world. Thus Dewey says that "qualities characteristic of sentiency are qualities *of* cosmic events" (*EN,* 204).

Not every experience that has aesthetic quality may be called an aesthetic experience. Whether it deserves the name "aesthetic experience" depends on the interest or purpose that controls its development. The felt qualities of, and relations among, things may be subordinated to a purpose beyond themselves—a scientific purpose, or one purely practical; or the felt qualities and relations may be seen as an end in themselves. Dewey concludes, "In as far as the development of an experience is *controlled* through reference to these immediately felt relations of order and fulfillment, that experience becomes dominantly esthetic in nature" (*AE,* 56).

In summation, all aesthetic experience is immediate, but not all immediate experience is aesthetic (*AE,* 123). An aesthetic experience is not a momentary or spontaneous one, though; it develops over time, and it involves at its last moment a fulfillment or closure of the felt relations of things in the experience, where that fulfillment or closure is itself the controlling purpose of the experience and is marked by a pervasive, qualitative whole.

Dewey compares and contrasts the adjectives "artistic" and "aesthetic" as a way of further clarifying his meaning. The contrast can be simply stated as one between the standpoint of the actor and that of the receiver. On the one hand, there is the activity of using materials to create a new object; on the other, there is "the delight that attends vision and hearing, an enhancement of the receptive appreciation and assimilation of objects irrespective of participation in the operations of production" (*EN,* 267). Dewey adds that disappointment might substitute for delight; the experience need not be a happy one in order to be aesthetic. But he is quick to assert that this distinction between aesthetic and artistic is not a hard and fast separation, since an artist engages in aesthetic perception during the process of creating a product, and since a truly artistic work is one designed for aesthetic perception. Moreover, the receptive stance of the person who appreciates art is not passive. In order to take in a work of art fully, or even to understand it at all, the spectator must engage in "an act of reconstructive doing" similar to that of the artist; the person who appreciates "must *create* his own experience" (*AE*, 59, 60). The similarities between the artistic and aesthetic processes lead Dewey to regret the lack of a common term to cover both (*AE*, 53).[6]

Dewey asserts that the artistic process is, above all else, an expressive one. This claim is typical of the late modern period in philosophy and in opposition to the ancients, who (to speak generally and roughly) had seen art as essentially an imitative process. In Plato's *Republic*, for example, the work of artists occurs at the lowest level on the divided line, as it deals only with images or representations of visible things, much less with forms. When Dewey says that the artistic process is expressive, he means that "the expression of the self in and through a medium, constituting the work of art, is *itself* a prolonged interaction of something issuing from the self with objective conditions, a process in which both of them acquire a form and order they did not at first possess" (*AE*, 71). The artistic process is not simply a matter of *self*-expression, as we have become accustomed to hearing the term used in the last few decades: the venting of one's feelings, without consideration of the circumstances. Dewey says felicitously that such behavior should be called "self-exposure" instead of "self-expression" (*AE*, 68). A truly expressive act, rather, is one that displays attention to the circumstances in which it occurs, as well as attention to purpose. The shaking of hands between partners in business to show sincerity fits this description, as does the shaping of marble into a statue by a sculptor. In any such case, according to Dewey, one can find at least the beginnings of art.

What the artistic process expresses is emotion; but an emotion is not "something existing somewhere by itself which then employs material through which to express itself" (*EN*, 292). It is fundamentally a person's reaction to objects encountered. Where it has no connection to an object it can be called an emotion only incipiently or abnormally. The object—in a case deserving of the name "art," the medium—serves to articulate the emotion. We deceive ourselves, however, according to Dewey, when we take the general names of an emotion such as love in such a way as to treat it as standing for a single feeling of which particular expressions are manifestations. What unifies the moments in an artistic or aesthetic experience is not a single emotion—a single experience may consist of a variety of emotions—but rather the presence of the pervasive qualitative whole that lends coherence to the different moments.

The second kind of common experience, the reflective, occurs because the felt qualities of things in immediate experience are not always in harmonious relation to one another; at times the feeling is one of disorder. Reflection arises upon the perception of disorder among the immediately felt things. It uses the material of immediate experience to form new objects, intellectual objects, in order to solve the problem. It begins with the qualities felt in immediate experience and forms relations among them. Reflection, once concluded, adds to future aesthetic experience: "Definiteness, depth, and variety of meaning attach to the objects of an experience just in the degree in which they have been previously thought about, even when present in an experience in which they do not evoke inferential procedures at all."[7] In other words, knowing about things enables us to experience them immediately in more meaningful ways.

We may infer from Dewey's theory of the relationship between immediate experience and reflective experience that reflection or science is typically not engaged in merely for its own sake. Dewey does realize that some people come to be interested in reflection for its own sake (and that such interest is to be welcomed, encouraged in those who show promise), but his general teaching is that it is engaged in for the sake of immediate experience. On a basic level, reflective conceptions are verified only by appeal to immediate experience, to the objects we encounter daily without thinking; without such reference scientific thinking is truly meaningless. Knowledge enables us to understand and then to control those objects. Moreover, reflection is necessary for the sake of aesthetic experience, both because it enhances meaning and because the aesthetic delight we find in something is possible only when juxtaposed to nonaesthetic experience (*EN*, 58).

The difference between immediate experience and reflective experience implies that not all things in a person's experience are objects of knowledge. Dewey remarks, "There are two dimensions of experienced things: one that of having them, and the other that of knowing about them so that we can again have them in more meaningful and secure ways."[8] By "having" here Dewey means feeling. He remarks, "Complex and active animals *have*, therefore, feelings which vary abundantly in quality. . . . They *have* them, but they do not know they have them" (*EN*, 198). The distinction can be put materially: "To become aware of an object cognitively as distinct from esthetically, involves external physical movements and external physical appliances physically manipulated" (*EN*, 284).

Moreover, Dewey claims that the experience of "having" or feeling a particular quality tells us as much about the real world as does the experience of knowing about it. Science has no privileged access to reality. Dewey's view is that a feeling of pain that has an external cause is as real as one that lacks an external cause. Scientific activity is privileged in the realm of knowledge, hence of truth; but the realm of reality is wider than that of truth.

Despite Dewey's distinction between reality and truth, we may doubt the exalted status of science when we are told that "having" certain qualities in experience tells us as much about reality as does knowing about them. We might be surprised to read Dewey making statements such as, "Science is an art." By "science" Dewey sometimes means an occupation, sometimes a body of knowledge. Here, however, he intends, as he usually does, not a body of information, but the method employed by scientists. He elaborates, "Knowledge or science, as a work of art, like any other work of art, confers upon things traits and potentialities which did not *previously* belong to them. Objection from the side of alleged [metaphysical] realism to this statement springs from a confusion of tenses. Knowledge is not a distortion or perversion which confers upon *its* subject-matter traits which *do* not belong to it, but is an act which confers upon non-cognitive material traits which *did* not belong to it" (*EN*, 285). This passage requires explanation. Dewey says that science confers traits on both "things" and "non-cognitive material." I do not believe that he is equating the two; rather he is writing from both sides of human experience, making the point incidentally that he elsewhere makes explicitly: human experience involves both processes internal to the person ("non-cognitive material") and things in the environment.

Dewey's experience-centered view holds that the scientific method is an active process, one that makes a transformation in the object known. Yet Dewey does not take the absurd position that the object of scientific investigation (e.g., a planet) is materially changed simply by undergoing investigation. Moreover, his view is not wholly unlike the traditional realist view. Thus he can write, "Scientific method or the art of constructing true perceptions is ascertained in the course of experience to occupy a privileged position in undertaking other arts"; yet he continues, "But this unique position only places it the more securely as an art; it does not set its product, knowledge, apart from other works of art" (*EN,* 284).

Contrary to Rorty's claim, the classification of science with the arts does not efface the difference between aesthetic experience and reflective activity. Yet Dewey sees something of the one in the other. "The [scientific] thinker has his esthetic moment when his ideas cease to be mere ideas and become the corporate meanings of objects" (*AE,* 21). Moreover, aesthetic experience—which, we must remember, is not a momentary happening—is partially constituted by scientific method; it is "the outcome of a skilled and intelligent art of dealing with natural things for the sake of intensifying, purifying, prolonging and deepening the satisfactions which they spontaneously afford" (*EN,* 291).[9]

It must be kept in mind, however, that aesthetic experience is not a special kind of experience. It is the paradigmatic form of meaningful experience in a world where humans strive for meaning. So Dewey writes that "esthetic experience is experience in its integrity. . . . For it is experience freed from the forces that impede and confuse its development as experience; freed, that is, from factors that subordinate an experience as it is directly had to something beyond itself. To esthetic experience, then, the philosopher must go to understand what experience is" (*AE,* 278). To say that reflective experience is paradigmatic, Dewey believes, would be to forget that from which it develops and that to which it ideally leads.

Artistic activity, we recall, differs from reflective activity in that it serves an extraneous purpose as well as exists for its own sake. Yet the extraneous purpose that art serves need not be a material or scientific one, as Dewey observes in discussing art at its pinnacle.[10] "The 'eternal' quality of great art," he writes, "is its renewed instrumentality for further consummatory experiences" (*EN,* 274). In other words, Dewey abides by the phrase "art for art's sake." "At their best," Dewey writes, products of art "assist in ushering in new modes of art and by education of the organs of perception in new modes of consummatory objects; they enlarge and enrich the world of human vision" (*EN,* 293). The matter may also be seen from the spectator's point of view, in terms of the aesthetic experience. Dewey states that "a genuinely esthetic object is not exclusively consummatory but is causally productive as well. A consummatory object that is not also instrumental turns in time to the dust and ashes of boredom" (*EN,* 274).

Dewey sees no absolute distinction between what is commonly called "fine" art and "useful" art. "[A]ll rankings of higher and lower [kinds of art] are, ultimately, out of place and stupid" (*AE,* 231). One may make a distinction of "rough practical value," he writes, between, say, a painting and an urn—the first of which is usually considered enjoyable in itself, the second enjoyable because of the use to which it can be put (*EN,* 283). In the case of the painting, however, appreciation of it may become a means to an end beyond itself; and, like the painting, an urn may be appreciated as beautiful in itself. Dewey concludes, "The only *basic* distinction is that between bad art and good art, and this distinction, . . . applies equally to things of use and of beauty." To make a sharp distinction between fineness and utility, he believes, would be ultimately to separate art from science so that the one has nothing to do with the other.

One scholar, J. E. Tiles, makes the pregnant suggestion, "On the surface Dewey's hostility to any absolute distinction between fine and useful art appears to be little more than a high-minded desire to bring refined and popular culture closer together, to 'democratize Art.' "[11] Tiles implies that useful art is the province of the people and fine art is the province of the leisure class. To "democratize art," then, would be to inject an element of thought or purpose into it beyond its present enjoyment (I do not mean that fine art is conceived thoughtlessly).

We gain a clearer understanding of Dewey's project in "democratizing art" by comparing and contrasting it with the view of art Socrates puts forward in Plato's *Republic.* In books 2 and 3 Socrates provides a critique of the arts from the standpoint of the practically wise. He subjects such arts as poetry and music to rational scrutiny and reaches conclusions as to what can and cannot be permitted in a well-ordered *polis.* Like Dewey, albeit for a different reason, he opposes the distinction between fine and useful art: any art worthy of praise must serve the

purpose of the *polis*. For both men fine art must conform to the requirements of thought; to use Dewey's terminology, it must have a place in
reflective as well as aesthetic experience. In one sense Plato can be said
to "democratize art": that of making art safe for the masses. For Plato,
however, this process would require compromising what the philosophers would find aesthetically worthy, whereas for Dewey no compromise as to the content of art is necessary. The root cause of this
difference, of course, is that for Plato only a few people at best are
capable of exercising sufficient reason to decide what art is worthwhile
and what is not; for Dewey the vast majority of people are capable of
developing the requisite intelligence.

DEWEY, POSTMODERN AESTHETICS, AND POLITICS

We are now prepared to proceed to the difficulty that I noted at the
beginning of this essay: whether Dewey can maintain his emphases on
both creativity and democracy. Here I shall compare and contrast Dewey
with Rorty and Lyotard—and then, more indirectly through Lyotard,
Immanuel Kant, and Edmund Burke.

In *Contingency, Irony, and Solidarity,* Rorty's denial of ahistorical
truth extends to a rejection of an ahistorical literary technique, the supposition of which leads to a false aestheticism "in which the aesthetic is
a matter of form and language rather than of content and life."[12] For
Rorty the aesthetic must be a matter of "content and life." As we have
seen, Rorty draws a sharp distinction between private and public spheres
and confines the uninhibited pursuit of self-creation to the former. In
different places throughout the book he makes the common aesthetic
distinction between the sublime and the beautiful. He credits Jacques
Derrida, who "privatizes the sublime," for realizing that "the public can
never be more than beautiful."[13] That statement suggests, however, that
the public can be beautiful, hence that the aesthetic is not to be wholly
excluded from the public sphere.[14] Indeed Rorty rejects the sharp division of moral and aesthetic (often accompanied by talk of conscience
and taste as separate faculties) because "that distinction merely blurs the
distinction I am trying to draw between relevance to autonomy and
relevance to cruelty."[15] The fundamental distinction for Rorty is between private and public, and works that are usually labeled "aesthetic"

can aid in the prevention of cruelty as readily as can works that are described as "moral." The crucial requirement for the public sphere is that aesthetic considerations not conflict with the goal of preventing cruelty.

Dewey would agree that moral judgments and aesthetic judgments cannot be rigidly separated, but for reasons somewhat different from Rorty's. As I explained in the previous chapter, according to Dewey objective moral judgments can be made, and they require to be made scientifically, which means experimentally. We may be aware of that fact in the sphere of politics, he says, but we tend to neglect it in what we wrongly consider the separate sphere of morals: "The real trouble is that there is an intrinsic split in our habitual attitudes when we profess to depend upon discussion and persuasion in politics and then systematically depend upon other methods in reaching conclusions in matters of morals and religion, or in anything where we depend upon a person or group possessed of 'authority' " (*FC,* 154). Dewey sees discussion and persuasion as essential to scientific method, as necessary aspects of the unique art that aims to build up true perceptions of the world around us. As we have seen, for Dewey all intellectual activity is artistic, hence also aesthetic.

But whereas both Dewey and Rorty refuse to separate aesthetics from morals, Dewey's fear of mixing aesthetic experience with politics is much less than Rorty's. For Dewey aesthetic experience is the paradigmatic form of meaningful experience, occurring when the controlling concern in experience is the immediately felt relation of order or fulfillment. That relation may obtain in political matters as well as in any other sort; in fact, we can consider aesthetic experience the goal of our attempts to solve our political problems, which arise when disorder is felt to occur. This helps to explain Dewey's opposition to the fragmentation of public and private conduct such as Rorty advocates.

Another reason for Dewey's willingness to mix aesthetic experience with politics may relate to the notion of the sublime briefly mentioned earlier concerning Rorty and Derrida. Since the seventeenth century, which saw the translation into English of the treatise traditionally called *On the Sublime* by the Greek critic Longinus (probably third century A.D.), the "sublime" has been a significant term in English literature and commentary. It is probably significant, then, that the term "sublime" does not figure importantly in Dewey's writing on aesthetics.

Indeed the term does not appear in the index to the critical edition of *Art as Experience* (unlike, e.g., "beauty" and "charm") or in the *Index* to Dewey's collected works.[16] I find only one use of "sublimity" in *Art as Experience,* which is to report the view of Denis Diderot (*AE,* 192). It is tempting to conclude that Dewey is unafraid to mix aesthetic experience and politics because he does not think in terms of the sublime.

But we must explore further this notion of the sublime in order to come to a fuller understanding of Dewey's view. In the work of Lyotard, arguably the most profound of postmodern writers, an emphasis on the sublime in art is immediately apparent.[17] His analysis draws on Burke's *A Philosophical Enquiry into the Origin of our Ideas of the Sublime and Beautiful.* Burke's original teaching on this subject links the sublime to pain and horror. According to Burke, "The passion caused by the great and sublime in *nature, when those causes* operate most powerfully, is Astonishment; and astonishment is that state of the soul, in which all its motions are suspended, with some degree of horror."[18] Later he qualifies the requisite state as "delightful horror."[19] "Delight" has a special meaning for Burke: in contrast with "pleasure," which is a positive feeling, delight is "the sensation which accompanies the removal of pain or danger."[20]

Burke claims that whatever produces the sublime "is productive of the strongest emotion which the mind is capable of feeling."[21] Lyotard comments, "For Burke, the sublime was no longer a matter of elevation (the category by which Aristotle defined tragedy), but a matter of intensification."[22] Lyotard notes in addition that Burke shows "that the sublime is kindled by the threat of nothing further happening."[23] Thomas Pangle has observed that for Lyotard, as for others, this threat or fear is rooted in "our greatest fear, the fear of violent death or of nothingness."[24] Thus, if we take Lyotard as our guide, we conclude that postmodern aesthetics is an effort to overcome this threat by intensifying the experiences had through art.

Although Dewey does not write on aesthetics in terms of the sublime, it is not as if he makes no mention of either elevation or intensification. He praises the work of Shakespeare and Keats, which "accepts life and experience in all its uncertainty, mystery, doubt, and half-knowledge and turns that experience upon itself to deepen and intensify its own qualities" (*AE,* 41). Any work of art, he says, is "the subject-matter of experiences heightened and intensified" (*AE,* 298).

The word that Dewey uses most often to refer to something like the sublime is "consummatory" or one of its forms. As we have seen, he writes of a series of events reaching a "consummation," "consummatory experience," and "consummatory objects." Wherever it is found, the consummatory involves a bringing to fulfillment or closure of the possibilities of experience. It produces in a person the sense that something, whether positive or negative, has been accomplished. But at the same time as it gives a sense of completeness, it may also bring a sense of incompleteness, pointing the way to a further series of events that will incorporate the former consummatory experience into another. Recall that great works of art do so, according to Dewey.

Yet the consummatory does not carry the connotation of elevation in Dewey's aesthetics.[25] The notion of the sublime as elevation implies that the state a person is trying to reach is *higher* than what he has achieved to that point. By contrast, for Dewey the consummatory is more of a bringing forth, a bringing out of. As Thomas Alexander puts it in his excellent book on Dewey's aesthetics, "The end of the work does not lie outside it but within it as a moving force, the entelechy rather than the terminus."[26] The "pervasive qualitative whole" that marks the consummatory and defines "*an* experience" is, Dewey observes, "felt as an *expansion* of ourselves" (*AE,* 199; italics added). Thus the consummatory cannot be realized by grasping, or even reaching for, something like a Platonic form that exists entirely above the visible world. Rather it involves development, the growing outward, of a self that already exists.

What does Dewey think about the sublime in the sense of intensification? To the extent to which aesthetic experience involves intensification for Dewey, it does not have the same root as Lyotard's notion of intensification: for Dewey the "fear of nothingness" does not seem to lie behind his desire to see experience intensified. In order to hold that Dewey's aesthetics are fundamentally similar to Lyotard's, one would have to show that he was moved by this fear. Now for most thinkers, the fear of nothingness has been prompted by the thought either that there is no God or that Aristotelian natural teleology is simply false and that there is no natural right or natural law in the sense in which, for example, Thomas Aquinas writes. Dewey's work is centrally influenced by these thoughts, but there is no evidence that he long remained in a condition of fear. He faces the prospect of a world absent final causes with optimism, not with dread. As I noted earlier, what enables him to do so is his conviction that he has found a way to reject moral absolutism while still avoiding moral subjectivism. Thus Dewey can say that human beings must "create new values" in a world where most of the old values have been formed without the help of scientific method, and he can still see that as entirely consistent with the employment of objective standards.

Now that we see why Dewey lacked a "fear of nothingness," what are the implications for politics of this difference between Lyotard's fear and Dewey's lack of it? I believe that the key is to be found in the notion of political enthusiasm, which appears in Lyotard's thought but not in Dewey's. Here Lyotard turns to Kant's *Critique of Judgment,* which draws on in part and rejects in part Burke's aesthetics.[27] Kant agrees with Burke that the sublime often accompanies feelings of astonishment and terror; but Kant denies Burke's claim that every source of fear is sublime, and Kant recognizes other feelings (such as admiration and reverence) as sources of the sublime. The latter difference, which amounts to a charge of oversimplification against Burke, is the more fundamental, and one where Dewey would surely agree with Kant.

Kant sees enthusiasm as the political effect of an emphasis on the sublime in art. It is the result of devotion to certain ideas on the part of people, a sort of devotion based on a sense, on the part of the observer, that a political event has absolute or universal meaning. The motivating ideas are thought to have universal significance. Enthusiasm manifests itself in unusually extreme political measures.[28] Intensification, which Lyotard stresses as well as Burke, can beget enthusiasm; and postmodernists deny the existence of any significant moral limits on political enthusiasm outside human convention.[29]

Intensification figures in Dewey's work, but enthusiasm does not, because Dewey thinks that the objects of aesthetic experience, objects having to do with values, are subject to the influence of scientific method. This is not to say that they are determined by experimentation and regulated in that way, but rather that Dewey believes that they cannot be preserved in experience for any significant duration unless the scientific method is employed to bring order out of the inevitable (at some time) perceptions of disorder among the things in prereflective experience. All the while, the object (in Dewey's terminology, the thing or event plus its meaning to a person) that is the focus of aesthetic experience will undergo modification, since science is transformative: the meaning, hence the object of aesthetic experience, will alter at least subtly in future experience. Moreover, the chance exists that it will be rejected entirely if found to be incompatible with an object thought to be more important. Here, then, is one reason why we might conclude that Dewey's emphasis on creativity and aesthetic experience would not have consequences deleterious to a democratic society.

A second reason has to do with Dewey's doctrine of historical relativism. He faults previous philosophers for failing to recognize that the conclusions they came to were not necessarily valid for all times or places. Premodern philosophers, he believes, thought that philosophy could disclose the truly real, once and for all. Early modern liberal thinkers too "had no idea of historic relativity, either in general or in its application to themselves."[30] If they had had such an idea, they would not have put forward a fixed doctrine of liberty; "they would have recognized that effective liberty is a function of the social conditions existing at any time."[31] Thus Dewey apparently does subscribe to some sort of historicism, defined as the claim that human thought cannot escape its time and place to reach universal principles.

Now recall that, for Kant, the way in which enthusiasm comes to have dangerous consequences involves a sense, on the part of the observer, that a political event has absolute or universal meaning. Yet Dewey's relativism rejects any claim to absolute meaning. Thus a true Deweyan would not see absolute or universal meaning in any political event.

To see a third reason we must recur to Dewey's lack of the "fear of nothingness" that lies behind Lyotard's project of intensification. The fact that, for Lyotard, intensification has its springs in the fear of nothingness is bound to affect the direction that the quest for intensification will take. If the root cause of intensification is a sense of almost despair, how likely can it be that people will avoid turning to desperate, and hence dangerous, measures in order to escape that sense and provide their lives with meaning; or else that they will passively resign themselves to a life of humdrum and become satisfied with bourgeois pleasures? When we look to the root of intensification according to Dewey, however, we find something very different, something more positive. Human beings find themselves in a situation where our transactions with one another and with the environment constitute meaning; if we live as we always have, we need not fear that there will be no meaning. What we seek is a more meaningful life than what we have, and we do so by deepening and intensifying those meanings that have already been established.

That difference leads to a fourth reason why we might be led to conclude that Dewey's emphasis on creativity would not harm democracy: Dewey encourages us to look for the aesthetic in the everyday affairs of modern society that postmodernists find boring and seek to escape more completely. Dewey's model is not the mechanic who has time to spend in dreamy contemplation admiring the object of his labors, but the mechanic who has a creative share in the intellectual decisions behind production and can thus fully appreciate the significance of his work (*AE*, 345–47). Dewey's famous concern to fashion liberal and vocational education to be more like each other aims to make the daily affairs of modern society less boring, but it is hard to see how they would not still be routine. If it is the "degree of completeness of living in the experience of making and of perceiving that makes the difference between what is fine or esthetic in art and what is not," then any sort of material is as fine as any other (*AE*, 33). Like Marx, Dewey believes that industrial and other business conditions are capable of being transformed into a fully socially rewarding environment.

CREATIVITY, THE LOSS OF THE SUBLIME, AND CIVIC EDUCATION

One of the themes found throughout Dewey's writings is the need for human beings "to create new ideals and values," as I noted before. Such talk would seem to invite people to become dissatisfied with "old values" and to alter their ways of life and institutions to suit new fashions. Democratic institutions and ways of thinking might be in danger from such an invitation. Dewey often claims for science a determinative role in this process of creating values; for example, he writes, "Take science (including its application to the machine) for what it is, and we shall begin to envisage it as a potential creator of new values and ends."[32] At other times he is more modest concerning the role that science can play, suggesting that it can help people to shape their purposes.

Whichever view is adopted, Dewey firmly believes that the process of creating values will not be dominated by aesthetic considerations, to the neglect of science. Recall his claim that aesthetic experience is "the outcome of a skilled and intelligent art of dealing with natural things" for the sake of increasing meaning and satisfaction; that art is science. The quest for aesthetic experience, for a certain feeling of order and fulfillment among the relations of things, should lead one to think. "Criticism is discriminating judgment, careful appraisal, and judgment is appropriately termed criticism wherever the subject-matter of discrimination concerns goods or values. Possession and enjoyment of goods passes insensibly and inevitably into appraisal" (*EN,* 298).

Here again we see how crucial Dewey's educational theory is to the overall success of his teaching. In order for aesthetic appreciation to pass "insensibly and inevitably" into appraisal, a person must have received an education along the lines of what Dewey recommends. The fundamental consideration is that science be "absorbed into imaginative and emotional disposition" (*DE,* 232). If it is not, the imagination will fly from one object to another guided only by the passion of the moment, moved after a while by boredom with each object. The solution to boredom, Dewey believes, is the ability to discriminate which objects are of greater worth and which are of lesser. That ability will produce a critical appreciation, a pleasure enhanced by the awareness that it is the result of a process of trial and that it will lead intelligently to another pleasure.

Particularly in discussions of civic education in his later years, Dewey also emphasizes the need for the "development of local agencies of communication and cooperation, creating stable loyal attachments, to militate against the centrifugal forces of present culture" (*FC,* 177). Democracy "will have its consummation when free social inquiry is indissolubly wedded to the art of full and moving communication"; and communication at its fullest, freest, and most effective occurs through works of art (*PIP,* 350; *AE,* 110, 249, 275, 291). A Deweyan society, then, would be one in which works of art—and remember that these works are not limited to fine art—have a central place in the conduct of politics, and at the local level where the meanings of those works of art may be more readily shared. (Dewey does not say so much on this point as we might like.)

Democratic or civic education means commitment to the shared method of observation, hypothesis, and judging by consequences of acting on hypothesis. But will democratic education legitimately do all for citizens that Dewey expects it to do? In chapter 2 we saw that Dewey anticipates the full integration of the good of the individual within the social good. I explained there, however, why I doubt that such integration will be forthcoming: The link between science and democracy is not so secure as Dewey thinks it is; and Dewey's psychology does not preclude the individualizing effects of his political theory. Thus if the goal is prevention of tyranny by the majority, I doubt that Deweyan liberalism will be an adequate substitute for rights-based liberalism. Dewey is confident that citizens will be sufficiently disciplined to maintain their appreciation for science. But it is questionable whether that will happen.

Part of that teaching is the claim that science provides unique access to truth, while Dewey also claims that the feeling of pain without an external cause is just as real as the feeling of pain with a verified external cause. A person's pain is real regardless of whether or not he can make a true statement about it. The word "truth" becomes relevant, however, only when a statement is made (1) that has meaning because of the consequences that follow upon acting on it and (2) that turns an indeterminate situation into a determinate one. For example, the statement "I have a pain in my stomach" is true if consequences attend that statement that one would expect. That distinction between truth and reality is so subtle that it has escaped some of Dewey's critics. The chances are significant that many average citizens would not be able to keep it in mind either. For many critics and for many in the public, the domains of truth and reality are coextensive. Thus some would ask, "If Dewey is correct that scientific method is not necessary for declaring a pain real, why is scientific method necessary for making a true statement about that pain?"

Dewey does not want the distinction between art (which deals with the domain of reality) and science (which deals with the domain of truth) to be "rubbed out," contrary to what Rorty says. But his claim "Science is an art," his attack on the correspondence theory of truth, and his historical relativism invite the view that he is an intellectual ancestor of postmodern political thought. Rorty's elaboration of public and private spheres involves the gamble that the private desire for self-creation will respect the public need to prevent cruelty, lacking any solid philosophical justification for that public goal. The success of Dewey's project likewise depends on the soundness of his optimism; if it is unsound, then the distinction between art and science will be erased. The view that science yields unique access to truth would then be overpowered by the postmodern claim that it is impossible to escape one's own perspective whether one is engaged in artistic expression or scientific experimentation.

One possible result of a weakened attachment to science is despair—the existentialist response to the acceptance of historical relativism. That despair could lead to two different responses. The first is the passive resignation of Nietzsche's "last man," a society of people who use bourgeois pleasures to cover their basic discomfort with their situation, in particular their inability to accomplish anything great with their lives. Accompanying this would likely be something similar to Tocquevillian "individualism." The outcome would surely not be a society of independent citizens capable of upholding a liberal democracy.

The second possible response is the opposite of passive resignation: a blind fervor expressing itself in dangerous political measures. Particularly if Dewey is correct that the essence of the artistic process, and hence partially of the aesthetic process, is expressing emotion, then an indulgence of the expression of emotion—even if a genuine emotion does, as Dewey says, have a connection to an object—would cloud the perception of disorder among the things we "have" by feeling; and the perception of disorder is necessary to provoke reflection or science. It is also necessary to promote political restraint.

The above possibilities assume that Dewey's doctrine of historical relativism will be accepted. The more likely scenario that must be considered, it seems to me, is that Dewey's doctrine of historical relativism will fail to gain widespread acceptance. Most people, most of the time, are not historical relativists. I do not wish to dispute arguments, made by such eminent thinkers as Allan Bloom in *The Closing of the American Mind,* that tolerance has become the leading virtue of Western civilization. But most people believe in God; most Americans and many Westerners affirm something like the inalienable human rights of the Declaration of Independence; and few people make important choices in their lives as if historical relativism were true, despite their exposure to relativistic teachings in schools. Moreover, to anyone who gives the matter much thought at all, that doctrine suffers from a problem with self-refutation in most or all of its forms.

It is probably safe to say that historical relativism has gained in influence in the last two centuries. But if what I have said above is true, then the likelier problem that must be considered is that absolutist attitudes will lead to political enthusiasm. When people see political events in terms of a struggle of ideas (a vision that it is usually provided by their political leaders), those events take on an absolute or universal meaning. Invested with such significance, those events may well meet with undemocratic responses. If the future of Western civilization is at stake in a war with Japan, then a majority of Americans may be expected to support internment of Japanese-Americans during wartime. The difficulty of maintaining the historical relativist position is seen in the fact that the survival of Western civilization was indeed at stake during World War II (and who would call Nazi or fascist "culture" the moral equivalent of Western civilization?); the difficulty with enthusiasm is seen in the overreaction that internment represented.

I contend that, given the character of Deweyan—i.e., pragmatic—liberalism and aesthetics, it cannot overcome those difficulties. I contend further that what Deweyan aesthetics lacks, above all else, is a notion of the sublime, particularly in the sense of elevation. We can see what is missing by turning to Longinus. In *On the Sublime* Longinus warns us not to be fooled by the appearance of elevation, or "the mere outward semblance of greatness."[33] He writes, "Any piece of writing which is heard repeatedly by a man of intelligence and experience yet fails to stir his soul to noble thoughts and does not leave impressed upon his mind reflections which reach beyond what was said, and which on further observation is seen to fade and be forgotten—that is not truly great writing, as it is only remembered while it is before us. The truly great can be pondered again and again; it is difficult, indeed impossible to withstand, for the memory of it is strong and hard to efface."[34] He continues, "The first characteristic of the sublime is its superiority in the penetrating force of its effect on the activities of intelligence . . . ; and the second characteristic is passion in its intensity and being-possessed."[35] According to Longinus, those are the two innate characteristics of great writers (there are others that can be acquired).

Now one of those two characteristics is intensification of passion. Lyotard says that intensification is featured in Burke's notion of the sublime, but we see that this quality did not originate in modern times. As I have noted, Dewey does speak of intensification in his writing on aesthetics.

But Dewey's teaching lacks mention of the first characteristic, which may be identified with elevation. When Longinus speaks of the sublime, his standard is the "man of intelligence and experience"; the sublime is what elevates the "activities of intelligence." Intensification may be a necessary condition of the sublime, but it is not a sufficient condition. Longinus even seems to imply that sublime writing points to something above itself: "noble thoughts," "reflections which reach beyond what was said," and "the activities of intelligence." Reason may seek something high and noble, and not the "more of the same" to which it would be limited if the sublime were conceived merely as intensification or neglected entirely.

Thomas Pangle makes the intriguing suggestion that, if we can recover something like Longinus' notion of the sublime, we might make possible a "rationalist 'aesthetics.'"[36] What would be the outlines of such an aesthetics? It is tempting to reach back to Plato's *Republic* for an answer and to say that what is deemed artistically or aesthetically worthy would be determined by a central authority of reason, which would decide on the basis of what is politically useful. But that response would be hasty; for one thing, it would be tantamount to saying that rationalist aesthetics is incompatible with liberal democracy. What rationalist aesthetics seems to mean at a minimum is that one's view of what is beautiful or artistically worthy should be informed by considerations of rationality. That view has nothing to say about politics, and rationalist aesthetics has nothing inherently to say about politics. We might add the stipulation that a beautiful work of art, or a beautiful anything else, is that which promotes a reasonable way of life. For example, Tocqueville refers to the American idea of rights as "beautiful" because it makes possible a free, but not licentious, society.[37] Liberal democracy allows for many answers to the question, "What is a reasonable way of life?"

But if liberal politics offers lofty possibilities as a form of government, as I believe that it does at its best, then we need to maintain a sense that some forms are loftier than others. As Pangle observes, "critical wonder and rational thought" constitute a necessary complement to Longinus' account of the elevated.[38] If what is sublime does not call forth a wonder that searches for the truth at the same time as it basks in the apparent beauty of the object of feeling, then it is not truly sublime at all.

Yet Dewey's historical relativism prevents such a search for the truth from occurring, *presupposing* as it does that absolute truth or meaning cannot be found in anything felt to be elevated or sublime. It teaches that our values or thoughts are in some measure determined by our historical situation, and it instructs us to consider that our values or thoughts are the result of a choice or commitment equal but not superior to another person's choice or commitment. It thus prevents the radical wonder that has inspired and fueled path-breaking developments in philosophy and science, and it prevents us from taking criticism of our choices and commitments seriously. Critical wonder and Deweyan historical relativism are incompatible.

Historical relativism dispels fear. It lowers the stakes and leads its adherents to believe that the choices they make are not of historic significance, so there is no need to be afraid of a bad choice. That is in keeping with the rest of Dewey's philosophy, with its message that human beings live in a world that is naturally meaningful and need not worry about a mythical abyss of meaninglessness. But does his insistence on driving away and keeping away fear serve Dewey well?

The traditional liberalism that Dewey seeks to replace relies on fear: the fear of losing one's life that is at the root of the individual rights of the state of nature. That fear leads Locke to devote his attention to preventing the worst-case scenario from happening. Deweyan political liberalism, not rooted in such fear, devotes little or no attention to the worst-case scenario. But if my argument in chapter 2 is correct, Deweyan liberalism does not provide satisfactory protection against tyranny of the majority. By not relying on fear, Dewey might be thought to promote a more courageous politics than traditional liberalism. But Locke's exhortation to courage is seen in his encouraging us to face our fear and use our political liberties.[39] The fear is present anyway, Locke would say; all we can do is not have it dominate our lives so openly. For Dewey there is, or should be, no fear to overcome.

A similar situation is found in aesthetics. As we have seen, postmodern aesthetics, at least as defined by Lyotard, is rooted partially in fear (Lyotard, drawing on Burke). That fear leads to a notion of the sublime in the sense of intensification. I am tempted to say that Deweyan aesthetics would do better to emulate postmodernism here, just as Dewey would do better to emulate traditional liberalism and its reliance on fear in his political theory. Although what is truly needed is a notion of the sublime in the sense of elevation, any account of sublimity might have a beneficial effect on political thinking.

Without an adequate protection of individual rights, those rights will not have widespread appreciation, and tyranny of the majority will not be sufficiently discouraged. But Deweyan constitutionalism is weak. The only adequate substitute for a strong, traditional, liberal constitutionalism, as I see it, is an account of the sublime, including elevation. That would help to provide a widespread appreciation for political forms. A "rationalist aesthetics," as Pangle suggests, is needed in order to bolster support for liberal democracy as the reasonable framework for reasonable ways of life.

It is possible that the recovery of the sublime in any sense would foster a political enthusiasm that would have dangerous results. But I believe that the potential benefit outweighs the risks. Ultimately, in order that liberal democratic politics might be stable and have the hope of being guided by wisdom, what we also need is an adequate understanding of science, especially political science, in its relation to philosophy.

NOTES

1. See, e.g., Friedrich Nietzsche, *Beyond Good and Evil* and *Ecce Homo*.

2. See Dewey, "Human Nature," 31, and "Does Human Nature Change?" 286–87.

3. Richard Rorty, "Priority of Democracy," 272.

4. One might conclude that Rorty himself is not fully postmodern here, since the prevention of cruelty trumps other considerations in his political thought. Nevertheless he seems to hold out hope that the activities of politics might be described as "beautiful." Rorty, *Contingency, Irony, and Solidarity,* 125.

5. Rorty, *Consequences of Pragmatism,* 51.

6. Dewey distinguishes between aesthetic and artistic as early as 1894. He writes then, "All the attacks, worth considering, of moralists upon art as meaning self-indulgence, effeminateness, corruption, etc., seem to me to rest on the confusion of artistic with aesthetic." John Dewey, *The Study of Ethics: A Syllabus* (1894), in E4 (1971): 301n19. In light of both his later insistence that no separation exists between the two terms and the fact that artistic creations are designed to have certain effects on their audience, I doubt that he can maintain this claim.

7. John Dewey, *Essays in Experimental Logic* (1916), in M10:329.

8. Dewey, *Experience and Nature*, 1st ed., 379. For an early statement of this important, much misunderstood distinction in Dewey's thought, see John Dewey, "The Postulate of Immediate Empiricism" (1903), in M3:158–67.

9. In his fine study of Dewey's aesthetics, Thomas Alexander observes that "the fulfillment of aesthetic experience as consummatory is really a 'postcognitive' rather than a 'precognitive' state. Experience is mediated by intelligence so that its meanings fuse and become funded in '*an* experience' which carries its critical, intellectual phase within the pervasively felt qualitative unity." Alexander, *Dewey's Theory*, 10.

10. The tendency to draw that conclusion was one reason why Dewey disliked the term "pragmatism" to refer to his thought as a whole and why he preferred "instrumentalism" to stress that science is instrumental to resolving a problematic situation.

11. J. E. Tiles, *Dewey* (London: Routledge, 1988), 189.

12. Rorty, *Contingency, Irony, and Solidarity*, 167.

13. Ibid., 125.

14. Rorty does not rest content with the separation of the private and public realms. He hopes that some critic will show how the works of Nietzsche the aesthete and John Stuart Mill the democrat can be joined to form a "beautiful mosaic" (ibid., 81). Rorty does not worry that his two materials may be incompatible, given a writer with a different intention from his.

15. Ibid., 142.

16. Anne S. Sharpe, ed., *Index to the Collected Works of John Dewey, 1882–1953* (Carbondale: Southern Illinois University Press, 1991).

17. My discussion of Lyotard is indebted to Thomas L. Pangle, *The Ennobling of Democracy: The Challenge of the Postmodern Age* (Baltimore: Johns Hopkins University Press, 1992).

18. Edmund Burke, *A Philosophical Enquiry into the Origin of our Ideas of the Sublime and Beautiful,* ed. James T. Boulton (London: Routledge and Kegan Paul, 1958 [1757]), 57.

19. Ibid., 73.

20. Ibid., 37.

21. Ibid., 39.

22. Jean-Francois Lyotard, "The Sublime and the Avant-Garde," trans. Lisa Liebmann, in *The Lyotard Reader,* rev. ed., ed. Andrew Benjamin (Oxford: Blackwell, 1989), 205.

23. Ibid., 204. See Burke, *Philosophical Enquiry*, 59, 131, 143.

24. Pangle, *Ennobling of Democracy*, 25.

25. The reference to "experiences heightened" is the only such sort of reference I have found in *Art as Experience* (*AE*, 298).

26. Alexander, *Dewey's Theory*, 212.

27. For a discussion, to which mine is indebted, see the introduction by James T. Boulton in Burke, *Philosophical Enquiry,* cxxv–cxxvii.

28. The French Revolution with its excesses is a famous example of enthusiasm. It is interesting to observe that Burke is a famous opponent of those excesses, despite the fact that his aesthetics involves a notion of the sublime as intensification.

29. Admittedly, as Harvey C. Mansfield reminds me, at the same time postmodernists deny the existence of any reason *for* enthusiasm.

30. Dewey, *Liberalism and Social Action,* 26.

31. Ibid., 27.

32. John Dewey, *Individualism, Old and New* (1930), in L5:118. For other references to the creation of values see *RP,* 122; "Individuality, Equality and Superiority" (1922), in M13:297; *Experience and Nature,* 4, 41; "Philosophy" (1928), in L3:123; *FC,* 167, 171–72.

33. Longinus, *On Great Writing (On the Sublime),* trans. G. M. A. Grube (Indianapolis: Hackett, 1991), 9.

34. Ibid., 9, 10.

35. Longinus, *On the Sublime,* quoted in Pangle, *Ennobling of Democracy,* 29, trans. Pangle.

36. Pangle, *Ennobling of Democracy,* 29.

37. Tocqueville, *Democracy in America,* 237.

38. Pangle, *Ennobling of Democracy,* 28.

39. This conclusion is suggested to me by a recent, unpublished paper by Harvey C. Mansfield, "Manliness and Liberalism."

5

ON DEWEY'S AND SOCRATES' CONCEPTIONS OF PHILOSOPHY

At the end of the previous chapter I claimed that the relation of Dewey's aesthetics to his political thought is cause for worry because Dewey's aesthetics lacks a notion of the sublime that can contribute to a rationalist aesthetics. In this chapter, to show how inadequacies in Dewey's thought should lead us to consider Socratic philosophy, first I bring out Dewey's understanding of science more fully than I have before; then I turn to his view of the relation between science and philosophy. That undertaking leads us to see the dogma at the root of Dewey's thought. That dogma weakens Dewey's significant attempt to provide a principled response to revealed religion and its political claims. Despite his protestations to the contrary, Dewey's own writings give evidence that philosophy is not merely the handmaiden to modern science. Then I examine Socratic dialectic and Dewey's response to it, suggesting that dialectic may enable us to reap the benefits of a tentative (as opposed to absolutist) philosophy without the disadvantages that follow from seeing modern science as the only way to truth.

SCIENCE AND PHILOSOPHY IN DEWEY'S THOUGHT

In chapter 3 I said that Dewey knows that modern science needs some explanation for itself, and I should begin by elaborating on that remark. Dewey insists that science is the sole avenue to truth. As we have seen, however, he is not a logical positivist. For logical positivists, science is the answer to the question of how we come to know anything—the answer that dispels all questions of value, relegating them to matters of emotion. Dewey rejects the dichotomy of facts and values and believes that it is possible to speak of moral facts, if we approach moral matters scientifically.

Perhaps Dewey is a naturalist who believes that talk of anything mental or spiritual can be reduced to physical terms. Such a view would explain why he does not have a notion of the sublime as elevated. For such a naturalist nothing is elevated in the normal sense of the word, because any great piece of writing or work of art can be fully accounted for in terms of the physical sciences. We may call that account "metaphysical materialism" or "materialist metaphysics," thus distinguishing it from materialist physics, because it is a grand philosophical view that claims that whatever is real can be described in physical terms.

Dewey is a naturalist. He never disdains that term. He does seek to clarify it, however, because he claims not to be a reductive naturalist or metaphysical materialist. In *Experience and Nature* he defines matter as "that character of natural events which is so tied up with changes that are sufficiently rapid to be perceptible as to give the latter a characteristic rhythmic order, the causal sequence. It is no cause or source of events or processes; . . . no principle of explanation; no substance behind or underlying changes" (*EN,* 65). Natural events are so complex that we should not be surprised to find a character in them that can be described appropriately only in material terms and another character that requires mental terms. "Nothing but unfamiliarity stands in the way of thinking of both mind and matter as different characters of natural events, in which matter expresses their sequential order, and mind the order of their meanings in their logical connections and dependencies" (*EN,* 66). Just as it is superstitious to believe that mind represents the essence of things while matter represents their existence, so the reverse is equally fanciful. "Historically speaking, materialism and mechanistic metaphysics—as distinct from mechanistic science—designate the doctrine that matter is the efficient cause of life and mind, and that 'cause' occupies a position superior in reality to that of 'effect' " (*EN,* 201). Both parts of that doctrine are false, Dewey claims: "[N]ot matter but the natural events having matter as a character, 'cause' life and mind. 'Effects,' since they mark the release of potentialities, are more adequate indications of the nature of nature than are just 'causes.' " In summary, Dewey remarks in a later essay, "while I believe Nature *has* a mechanism . . . I do not accept its *reduction* to a mechanism."[1]

Dewey does not completely reject materialism. Scholar W. H. Sheldon wrote a critique of naturalism claiming that naturalism is coextensive with materialism in which physical laws rule the behavior of an organism and provide the sole explanation of change in an organism.[2] Dewey denies that claim, but he admits that, in a sense, he is a materialist. If materialism is the proposition that mental qualities "are not additional things which are *substantially* distinct from the properties and behaviors of spatio-temporal objects in their organized unity," then he is a materialist.[3] Yet here too he is careful to distinguish his naturalistic materialism from the usual variety: science is not the only valid or meaningful way to encounter the world. Sheldon claimed that we should not rule out the possibility of finding truth in matters commonly referred to as supernatural, but Dewey will not go so far. "The *horror supernaturae* with which Mr. Sheldon not unjustly charges the naturalists is . . . not a capricious rejection on their part of well-established beliefs: it is a consequence of their refusal to accept propositions, like the belief in ghosts, for which the available evidence is overwhelmingly negative."[4] In other words, naturalists do bristle at the thought of the supernatural, but that is the effect of their adherence to scientific method, not the cause of their adherence to it.

If we are to believe Dewey, then, his naturalism is free from any taint of metaphysical materialism. If one reads Dewey carefully, however, evidence to the contrary can be found. One of the reasons he gives for the progress made by modern science over premodern science is that the former no longer searches for single, all-encompassing laws and contents itself with a plurality of laws and beings (*FC*, 123). That statement is not simply true, nor was it true during Dewey's lifetime. In numerous cases scientists look for single, underlying laws, causes, or forces. For example, physicists have detected four fundamental forces of nature (gravitational, electromagnetic, strong nuclear, and weak nuclear); yet a number of physicists continue to search for a single force underlying those four. Like many people, physicists desire simplicity and elegance in their work; those "values" lead them to undertake the research that they do. Dewey should not be surprised at that. Would he say that those physicists are wrongly influenced by religious sentiment?

We must ask why Dewey makes the unproven statement that science is uninterested in ultimate causes. Perhaps he is unintentionally seeking to democratize the conclusions of science.[5] If science were to uncover a single, all-encompassing law, that law might be thought anti-pluralistic; and political thinkers seeking to draw lessons from science and nature could reach antidemocratic conclusions. Alternatively, perhaps, despite his protestations to the contrary, he is under the influence of a materialism that seems to have roots in an antitheological passion. The antitheological passion has led scientists to make such unfounded, dogmatic statements as "Science will never be able to uncover the cause of the Big Bang" and "Science will never be able to tell us anything about a divinity," thus discouraging other scientists from giving those questions attention; and Dewey may be reflecting the same sort of antipathy toward thinking about ultimate causes. Moreover, in *Experience and Nature* Dewey goes beyond explaining that mental processes are linked to physical ones; he asserts that minds work according to a mechanism. "Every discovery of concrete dependence of life and mind upon physical events is therefore an addition to our resources. If life and mind had no mechanism, education, deliberate modification, rectification, prevention and constructive control would be impossible" (*EN,* 201). This passage shows, it seems to me, that Dewey may be swayed by a metaphysical materialism despite his conscious rejection of it.

I make that claim despite some further evidence to counter the charge of reductive naturalism. Contemporary scientists usually have a difficult time with the term "soul"; either they are reductive naturalists themselves, or (if they have not thought so much about philosophical questions) the word "soul" simply has religious associations that make it unfit for serious discussion. But not only does Dewey have no antipathy toward the term "soul"; he almost insists on its scientific validity. Soul

> denotes the qualities of psycho-physical activities as far as these are organized into unity. Some bodies have souls preeminently as some conspicuously have fragrance, color, and solidity. . . . Were there not in actual existence properties of sensitivity and of marvelously comprehensive and delicate participative response characterizing living bodies, mythical notions about the nature of the soul would never have risen. . . . [T]he idiomatic non-doctrinal use of the word soul retains a sense of the realities concerned. To say emphatically of a particular person that he has soul or a great soul is not to utter a platitude, applicable equally to all human beings. It expresses the conviction that the man or woman in question has in marked degree qualities of sensitive, rich and coordinated participation in all the situa-

tions of life. Thus works of art, music, poetry, painting, architecture, have soul, while others are dead, mechanical. (*EN,* 223)

That passage shows Dewey's courage in more ways than one. First, he claims that the existence of the soul is fact. Second, he argues that human beings are not all equal in terms of soul. Coming from him, that argument is particularly surprising because of its apparently undemocratic character.

He also writes of spirit: "Animals are spirited, but man is a living spirit. He lives in his works and his works do follow him. Soul is form, spirit informs. It is the moving function of that of which soul is the substance" (*EN,* 224). But he does not have great hope that we can begin to use the terms "soul" and "spirit" without their traditional, supernatural connotations; and he concedes that the terms may have to be abandoned, without conceding that the things they represent are any less real.

What can we make of Dewey's use of the term "soul"? In a word, I believe, it is impoverished. He is intent to describe, and give a label to, something about human beings that cannot be captured by talking about mass in motion, and we should not blame him for that. Nor should we blame him for being unable to give a definition that avoids all controversy. Yet a look at his description of the soul reveals two instances of the words "sensitive" and "participation," or forms thereof. "Participation" is a generic word, indicating a taking part in something, without specifying what is worth taking part in; social scientists often speak of participation, political or otherwise, to include everything from voting to running for political office. Everyone participates in something; but who would want to participate in "all the situations of life," as if all situations we find ourselves in were equally worth our "rich participation"? "Sensitivity" is a leading modern virtue; but its very mention does not answer the question, To what should we be sensitive? Dewey's account of the soul seems to want to describe something elevated, worth striving for; but it is instead remarkably flat.

If we want to find an account of the soul that describes something elevated apart from the religious associations disdained by Dewey, we might turn to ancient philosophy. That is not an option for him, because of its allegedly unscientific character. We need to discern what he sees as the relation between philosophy and science. In order to do that, we must first study the two senses in which Dewey conceives of philosophy.

In the first sense Dewey writes of philosophy as intellectual activity. If it does not lead by itself to knowledge, at least it clears the way for that quest. Philosophy is not a theory of the relation between theory and practice, but merely "an intellectual pursuit" the status of which "signifies nothing beyond the fact that those who engage in it should respect the canons of fairness, impartiality, of internal consistency and external evidence" (*QC,* 55). Historically, according to Dewey, philosophy arose from conflict in ancient Greece between a ruling class that controlled the myths all people were expected to respect and a working class that was responsible for advances in knowledge in more mundane matters. It has since been chiefly concerned with disputes between old institutions and new tendencies. When we realize this, "it will be seen that the task of future philosophy is to clarify men's ideas as to the social and moral strifes of their own day" (*RP,* 94). Philosophy does not itself attain knowledge, but it prepares a path for the acquisition of knowledge. In order to do so, it "must assume a practical nature; it must become operative and experimental" (*RP,* 149).

This sense of philosophy is opposed to a conception of philosophy as settled theory that explains man's relations with other beings and his place in the universe. The uniqueness of aesthetic experience, Dewey claims, is "a challenge to that systematic thought called philosophy. For esthetic experience is experience in its integrity. . . . [Aesthetic experience is free] from factors that subordinate an experience as it is directly had to something beyond itself" (*AE,* 278). (Note here the distinction between an experience that is "had" and one that is "known.") Dewey suggests that while systematic thought can be called philosophy, it is not truly so.

Yet in important books, Dewey seems to write of philosophy as if it were systematic theory. In his main book on education he calls it "*the general theory of education,*" where education is "the process of forming fundamental dispositions, intellectual and emotional, toward nature and fellow-men" (*DE,* 338; italics in original). In his main book on metaphysics he calls it "a generalized theory of criticism," "a criticism of criticisms," which "continuously provides instruments for the criticism of those values—whether of beliefs, institutions, actions or products— that are found in all aspects of experience" (*EN,* 9, 298). Elsewhere he refers to it as "the theory of the practice, through ideas sufficiently definite to be operative in experimental endeavor, by which the integration [of knowing and doing] may be made secure in actual experience"; philosophy must "develop a system of operative ideas congruous with present knowledge and with present facilities of control over natural events and energies" (*QC*, 204, 226).

There is a tension, if not a contradiction, between the two afore-mentioned senses of philosophy that should not be overlooked. Philosophy as an intellectual activity or pursuit is philosophy in its original sense, the Greek sense of a love of wisdom and a seeking after wisdom. It is not necessarily the attainment or possession of wisdom. Yet, if engaged in steadily, it may become a way of life. Socrates, in Plato's *Apology of Socrates* and elsewhere, reminds us of the limits to his wisdom while showing us how he pursues it. He reminds us that human opinions or theories can always be questioned, suggesting that a full attainment of wisdom is beyond human reach. Philosophy as intellectual activity thus seems incompatible with philosophy seen as a theory, whether theoretical explanation of education, metaphysics, politics, or anything else.

Yet Dewey appears to consider those two senses of philosophy compatible. Immediately after defining philosophy as "the generalized theory of education," he calls it "a form of thinking" (*DE*, 341). Shortly after calling philosophy a "theory of criticism," he says that is "a version of the old saying that philosophy is love of wisdom, of wisdom which is not knowledge and which nevertheless cannot be without knowledge" (*EN*, 305). Are those two senses of philosophy inconsistent? One might argue with Dewey that they are not: Philosophy as theory implies possession of wisdom or knowledge; but philosophy as pursuit of wisdom does also—at least knowledge of the important questions to ask. That knowledge may be expressed in theory, as long as that theory is subject to revision, in a way that is compatible with a conception of philosophy as intellectual activity or way of life. The key point for Dewey is that the theory should be revised in light of the best current evidence.

I am not at all sure that Dewey's argument for compatibility of those two senses of philosophy—if that is what his argument would be—is a strong one. Let us concede that it is conclusive, however, and examine what Dewey sees as the relation between philosophy and science. The obstacle to conceiving of philosophy in those two senses, as Dewey sees it, is the traditional view of philosophy. "It has . . . claimed that it was in possession of a higher organ of knowledge than is employed by positive science and ordinary practical experience, and that it is marked by a superior dignity and importance" (*RP*, 92). Socrates and Plato sought to reconcile the imaginative beliefs that governed Athens with the more mundane knowledge of the artisans by finding a sound basis for morals in metaphysics, as opposed to custom. According to Dewey, this project of replacing custom with metaphysics is "the leading theme of the classic philosophy of Europe, as evolved by Plato and Aristotle" (*RP*, 89). This metaphysics held that what is truly real is ideal, nonmaterial, atemporal, changeless; the inferior kind of being is the opposite of those qualities, accessible to observation by the senses. It follows that knowledge at its highest level is contemplative, not practical; hence we arrive at the dichotomy of theory and practice. The task of philosophy became the disclosure of the truly real and the attainment of certainty, through the building of system; this building was to be accomplished by the use of reason freed from passion. Disclosure of the truly real would provide guidance in practical affairs. But ancient philosophy failed to convince that it had arrived at the desired certainty. It could not have succeeded, says Dewey, because its project was misconceived.

Instead, according to him, philosophy must (1)renounce belief in antecedent Being, (2)make clear what revisions are needed in traditional judgments about values, and (3)project "ideas about values which might be the basis of a new integration of human conduct"—integration, that is, of conduct stemming from scientific beliefs with conduct stemming from beliefs about values (*QC*, 37). Philosophy should have a part in a reconciliation of facts and values, but it must first humble itself and recognize its limitations. A proper "reconstruction" of philosophy "will regard intelligence not as the original shaper and final cause of things, but as the purposeful energetic re-shaper of those phases of nature and life that obstruct social well-being" (*RP*, 108). Such a reconstruction will leave aside speculation about an original shaper and a final cause, because scientific method cannot answer those questions.

In ancient times philosophy and science were more closely related—even synonymous in some cases—than they are today.[6] In Dewey's eyes they are surely not synonymous: "Philosophy as itself science is a humbug and played out. But take all the science there is, and there is a question: What is its bearing on the conduct of life—not in detail, but with reference to general lines of policy forming—using the word policy to apply to the relatively more comprehensive ends by means of which activities hang together over a period of time and a fairly wide human area."[7] Thus he believes that philosophy and science are not so closely related today as they should be: we must respect the findings of science and their application in technology not only in a certain sphere, but also in the spheres of religion, morals, and politics; and philosophy must search for values, for the uses to which science and technology should be put (*QC*, 248).

A proper appreciation of science requires understanding that practice is not for the sake of theory, nor is theory for the sake of practice. (The object is said to be "social well-being," a Deweyan phrase I suggest we cannot understand without reference to his analyses of growth and aesthetic experience.) Philosophy must follow the lead of science, always respecting its findings. Philosophy must not forget its history: the motive for philosophy is "the need of reconciling the moral rules and ideals embodied in the traditional code with the matter-of-fact positivistic knowledge which gradually grows up" (*RP*, 85). Thus its conclusions are to be limited by its task of having to adjust a traditional moral code to the realities of present-day life. Philosophy is observation of and reflection on actual conditions to discern their meaning. It must offer hypotheses that are "projections of the possibilities of facts already in existence and capable of report" (*QC*, 63).

Dewey's metaphysics is an attempt to fulfill that requirement. It is an effort to identify "generic traits of existence" on the basis of what science reveals to us about existence. Those generic traits are hypotheses, statements about what we can expect to find when we encounter things: repetition, variableness, safety, hazardousness. This metaphysics is not itself what is normally called moral philosophy, but Dewey insists on its connection to other branches of philosophy. It is when "experience actually presents esthetic and moral traits" that "these traits may also be supposed to reach down into nature, and to testify to something that belongs to nature as truly as does the mechanical structure attributed to it in physical science. . . . When found, their [i.e., that of the "traits possessed by the subject-matters of experience"] ideal qualities are as relevant to the philosophic theory of nature as are the traits found by physical inquiry" (*EN*, 13–14). Metaphysics, as "theory of nature," is as concerned with the making of moral judgments by human beings as it is with their making of tools (something controlled by humans) or with the change of seasons (something not under their control).

On his view, Dewey's metaphysics is no more to be considered timeless truth than the rest of his teaching. It is particularly important for our purposes to note the close connection that Dewey sees between the scientific method and historical relativism. "The fundamental defect" of early political liberalism, says Dewey, "was its lack of perception of historic relativity."[8] It did not realize that the notion of the individual in the state of nature could be used to stifle political liberty as well as to promote it; that happened when advocates of laissez-faire in economics attacked governmental intervention for the sake of the poor. "Ideas that at one time are means of producing social change have not the same meaning when they are used as means of preventing social change. This fact is itself an illustration of historic relativity." Science has taught us the lesson that the meaning and validity of ideas and principles vary with the purposes to which they are put. Thus Dewey claims, "The connection between historic relativity and experimental method is intrinsic." Since philosophy must bow to science, it cannot challenge the teaching of historical relativism but must adhere to it.

If Dewey's teaching were accepted, its effect on philosophy would be considerable. It would surely diminish the wonder that is at the root and heart of philosophy—certainly philosophy in the first of the two senses mentioned above and sanctioned by Dewey, that of intellectual activity. With a sense of the eternal blotted out by the doctrine of historical relativism, there would be less for the human mind to wonder at. Many philosophers (perhaps even all worthy of the name) have asked whether there are eternal truths, whether human thought can transcend its time and place; historical relativism has been a position that they have pondered. Some of them have thought historical relativism impossible because it is self-refuting when stated definitively. But Dewey considers the question settled, at least as settled as the worth of the scientific method.

As for the worth of science, Dewey seems halfway open to questioning it. The experimental philosophy of life "is itself a theory to be tested by experience."[9] But by what sort of experience, by what standards can we tell the worth of science, which is then to be applied toward the making of all other moral judgments? Elsewhere, he writes that the experimental attitude toward life "is clearly a faith, not a demonstration. It too can be demonstrated only in *its* works, its fruits." But again, demonstrated by what standards? Then Dewey hedges. "Perhaps the task is too hard for human nature. The faith may demonstrate its own falsity by failure. . . . But an honest soul will also admit that the failure is not due to inherent defects in the faith, but to the fact that its demands are too high for human power; . . . and that the experiment must be passed on to another place and time."[10] Dewey is unwilling to conclude that the worth of modern scientific method for arriving at the truth of things is timelessly limited in comparison with some other sort of intellectual activity. Apparently, his historical relativism, rather than being derived from science, determines the conclusions he will draw about science. Dewey is beginning to look more dogmatic.

When Dewey uses the word "dogma," it is usually in a pejorative manner. What he means by the term is the same as, or not far from, the standard meaning of a fixed tenet. This opposition is understandable, because dogmatism is opposed to his pragmatism or instrumentalism, which treats thought and action as means toward the enrichment of experience (in particular the achievement of aesthetic experience) and which considers all truths tentative. One exception to this usage is a dialogue with George Santayana, who called himself a "dogmatic naturalist."[11] Dewey does not blame Santayana for his dogmatism because "everyone, in my conception, must be dogmatic at some point in order to get anywhere with other matters."[12] What Dewey apparently means is that judgment on a hypothesis can remain suspended for only so long; then action must occur, and the hypothesis must be treated as fixed and authoritative, at least for the purpose of that action. He also means that we may have to make certain assumptions in order to form a hypothesis.

But Dewey would insist that those assumptions be questioned at some other time. If they were not, they would effectively be absolutes in a person's thought. The point I wish to make is that the principle of historical relativism does serve as absolute in his thought, that he never fully seems to question it. Thus, by Dewey's own standards, to a significant extent he is a dogmatist.

This dogmatism of Dewey's hinders his ability to provide a satisfactory response to other instances of dogmatism. Today one of the most important examples of political claims based on dogmas—and one of the most challenging to deal with—is that of revealed religion. Dewey's dogmatism hinders his ability to explain whether or why we are in need of a theoretical or practical response to the claims of revealed religion, or to provide such a response. This is a point worth examining in some detail.

THE POLITICAL EFFECT OF DEWEY'S DOGMATISM

When Dewey began his philosophical career in the 1880s he was a neo-Hegelian idealist, defending an ethical philosophy according to which the individual consciousness of a human being is in the service of an absolute consciousness, and the study of human consciousness is a means to the study of the absolute. During the 1890s he moved away from idealism and toward the pragmatism for which he is known, because he saw no need for any notion of *Geist* or another Absolute in an understanding of human experience. To the best of my knowledge, Dewey never links the issue of the Absolute to the question of the truth or falsity of Christianity; but it appears likely that the two matters were related for him, because references to God in his work become infrequent after that time, and because over the course of dozens of books and hundreds of articles, Dewey fails to devote lengthy, explicit attention to the question of divine revelation. Even *A Common Faith,* his major work on religion, does not ask and consider whether the God of the Bible exists. Dewey later says that that book was addressed specifically to those who already reject supernatural religion.[13]

When we ask how Dewey treats claims concerning revealed religion, we must consider two sorts of claims: theological or theoretical, and political or practical. Dewey deals with theoretical claims concerning revelation by submitting them to scientific method; their validity is to be determined by their ability to render a problematic situation unproblematic. He asks whether the consequences of those claims solve the dilemma that prompted the asking of the question.

Now this does not mean the disparagement of all of the substance of religion as nonsense, as one might expect from him. In *A Common Faith* Dewey draws a distinction between religions, which science has shown to be false, and religious experience, which has validity. We must see religions as relative to cultures—and hence their aspiration to represent eternal truth as misguided—and instead seek "the ways in which reverence and obedience would be manifested, if whatever is basically religious in experience had the opportunity to express itself free from all historic encumbrances"—that is, institutional encumbrances.[14] Religious experience occurs within, and cannot occur apart from, aesthetic, scientific, moral, or political experience. "The way in which the experience operated, its function, determines its religious value"; here we can see the application of the scientific test of consequences.[15] Religious experience refers to "the attitudes that lend deep and enduring support to the processes of living"; there is where reverence may properly be shown.[16] A religious attitude is comprehensive, recognizing the dependence of man upon nature. According to Dewey, faith in obtaining truth through continual inquiry into man's natural situations is more religious than faith in obtaining truth through revelation: the fact of competing alleged revelations demands empirical investigation, he suggests, and empirical inquiries into the supernatural divert attention from realizing our ideals. Dewey's belief in the religiosity of scientific inquiry is seen in his willingness to use the term "God" for "the unity of all ideal ends arousing us to desire and actions," although he says that it is only for the benefit of those who would otherwise despair or feel isolated.[17]

The foregoing shows that Dewey's scientific treatment of religion in general, and of revealed religion in particular, does not aim to be value-neutral. The purpose of such treatment is to sort those statements about ideals that are comprehensive and that admit man's dependence on nature from those statements that do not. Science is not a neutral instrument; it arises from prereflective experience, works with objects derived from prereflective experience, and leads to an enrichment of unreflective experience. That is a value-laden process, as Dewey sees it.

Nor does Dewey deal with the political claims of revealed religion in a value-neutral manner. Those proposals may concern the injustice of abortion or capital punishment or the need to redistribute wealth to accord with human dignity. Dewey's political theory, as we saw it in chapter 2, sets forth two standards for judging those proposals: First, the state should prevent negative consequences of actions that affect people beyond those directly concerned; it should prevent harm. Second, the state should encourage positive developments; it should foster growth. Dewey's liberalism is one that takes an active role in promoting the common good. In order to do that, it must take sides, and Dewey does not shrink from doing so.

Because his liberalism is not value-neutral, his treatment of religion is not open to one charge that is commonly made against liberalism, a charge made forcefully by Stanley Fish in an article entitled "Liberalism

Doesn't Exist."[18] Responding to an article by Stephen Carter in which Carter argues for a liberalism appreciative of religion, Fish says that such politics are impossible, because "liberalism is informed by a faith (a word deliberately chosen) in reason as a faculty that operates independently of any particular world view."[19] The quarrel between reason and religion is a false one, Fish says, because reason—that is, recourse to empirical verification to arrive at truth—rests on belief just as much as does religion. The real quarrel is between beliefs, two incompatible assumptions or premises. Liberalism is not truly a neutral instrument that can impartially adjudicate between competing claims; it is itself a faith, a belief in reason, that is inherently hostile to the claims of religion, which wants to arrive at truth by means of divine revelation. Liberalism is "tolerant only *within* the space demarcated by the operations of reason. . . . A liberalism that did not 'insist on reason as the only legitimate path to knowledge about the world' [which is what Carter wants] would not be liberalism; the principle of a rationality that is above the partisan fray (and therefore can assure its 'fairness') is not incidental to liberal thought; it *is* liberal thought, and if it is 'softened' by denying reason its priority and rendering it just one among many legitimate paths, liberalism would have no content."[20] Yet it is precisely Fish's claim that such neutrality is impossible, because the liberal claim that "reasons come from nowhere, that they reflect the structure of the universe or at least of the human brain" is "in fact" false (has Fish found neutrality here in rejecting this liberal claim, or is use of "in fact" merely shrewd rhetoric?).[21]

The difference between Dewey and Fish is instructive, in part because it shows how liberal theory has changed even since Dewey's day, in part because it aids in showing his similarities to and differences from postmodernism. Dewey would dispute Fish's claim that the essence of liberal thought is a rationality apart from a moral or political agenda. For Dewey the very aim of liberalism is to promote ends deemed moral at the expense of those deemed immoral. Nor would he agree with Fish that the *real* essence of liberalism, in contrast with its stated purpose, is "a very particular moral agenda (privileging the individual over the community, the cognitive over the affective, the abstract over the particular)."[22] According to Dewey, the agenda of liberalism is the proper situating of the individual within the community, a recognition that the two are not separate entities but that one needs the other if it is to realize its full potential. Yet Dewey does not reject what Fish appears to see as the premise of his claim about the real liberalism: Dewey does not deny that reasons come from "somewhere" and not from "nowhere," to use Fish's terms. If we take Fish literally, I know of no philosopher who does believe that reasons come from "nowhere"; but if we try to understand his intent, we realize that Dewey certainly does not agree with, say, Kant about the possibility of pure practical reason. For Dewey reason—or "intelligence," as he prefers to say—always involves empirical information. Where Dewey disagrees with Fish again is in saying that liberal thought *requires* that reasons come from nowhere. Neither early liberals such as Hobbes and Locke, nor later liberals such as Kant and Mill, with their "absolutist" claims, made that pronouncement. Fish's conception of liberalism owes much to that of John Rawls, who in *A Theory of Justice* and *Political Liberalism* has claimed to be neutral with respect to "comprehensive religious, philosophical, and moral doctrines."[23]

Deweyan liberalism, like earlier liberal theories, claims that it can be at least somewhat above the partisan fray without being morally neutral. It can command a position of respectability among all reasonable citizens through recourse to the scientific—that is, democratic—method of settling disagreements. Deweyan liberalism will take sides, though, as I remarked earlier, because not all arguments advanced by citizens will be deemed equally conducive to growth.

Yet, as we have seen, Deweyan liberalism has its own dogmatic basis. In a society organized on Deweyan principles, if a believer in a religious fundamentalism were to ask why he or she should submit to having a political dispute settled by scientific method, the public response—if we are to judge from Dewey's writings—would manifest an unwillingness to countenance anything other than modern science as offering the way to truth, a refusal based on an assumption of historical relativism. The dispute between the Deweyan public or state and the religious fundamentalist comes down in the end to a difference of dogmas. Why should one prevail over the other? Dewey's assumption of historical relativism is at least as questionable as some assumptions made involving revealed religion (e.g., that a God exists). On what philosophical ground can it be said that the differing dogmas should not try to coexist, to work out some sort of compromise, instead of abiding a winner-take-all result? Dewey does not appear to provide a nonarbitrary ground. Surely he does not see life as a struggle for power and defend the coercive policy of the state on that basis. Thus, regardless of our beliefs about religious matters, we should not be satisfied with the reply of Deweyan liberalism to the claims of revealed religion.

Of course, an objection might be made that it is fruitless to seek a nonarbitrary ground for a philosophical position, so that the demand made on Dewey is unreasonably harsh. That objection must be given considerable weight. An initial rebuttal to it would be that, even if the objection were correct, it does not follow that all philosophical grounds are equally arbitrary. Thus we would not be misguided to look for a less arbitrary liberalism than the one Dewey gives us. But the objection goes deeper by asking what we should be prepared to settle for as a philosophical basis or context for liberalism. Is it possible to give a nonarbitrary or nondogmatic (those are not necessarily synonyms but at least closely related) philosophical defense of liberalism? Is a nonarbitrary or nondogmatic philosophy possible? In this book on Dewey I cannot give a complete answer to those questions, even if I were fully confident of the answer. I can, however, suggest an alternative, and examine the scope of Dewey's differences with it.

As I remarked earlier, Dewey's claims that science is no longer desirous of finding ultimate causes and that the human mind has a mechanism seem to drift toward or even reflect an unintentional metaphysical materialism. He wants to subscribe to a scientific method without adopting the philosophical positions that often accompany it; but it appears he is unable to do so. Perhaps he is simply slipping into unwarranted speculation; or perhaps something in him sees a need to consider those ultimate questions that he claims we can and should leave behind. If I am correct here, this teaches us that ultimate questions are not so easily avoided as Dewey believes or as we often think.

These lapses, if lapses they are, may make us wonder whether the relation that Dewey envisions between philosophy and science is feasible. For that relation has philosophy as the handmaiden to science. How easily does philosophy accept that relationship? From Dewey's own example, it appears not so easily: Deweyan philosophy goes to exactly the question about ultimate causes—presupposing an answer to it—that Deweyan science claims is uninteresting. Can philosophy exist in that relationship with science? It might be said that the modern philosophical project is in effect an attempt to answer that question. We may at least wonder whether philosophy can be "taken down a notch" so easily as

Dewey thinks. Or is there something in philosophy, or in the human mind, that resists such humbling (not to say humiliation)?

We have already looked briefly in this chapter at the notion of philosophy as intellectual activity or a way of life. Let us now examine it in more detail as a possible alternative to Deweyan philosophy, as a possible exemplar of the nonarbitrary, nondogmatic philosophy about which we asked.[24]

SOCRATIC DIALECTIC AND DEWEY'S RESPONSE TO IT

As far as we know, the notion of philosophy as a way of life (although not philosophy simply) originated with Socrates as presented in the dialogues of Plato; so it is proper to devote most of our attention to Socratic philosophy. It is dialectic that Socrates intends by philosophy. In the *Phaedrus* he describes it as the activity of distinguishing particulars according to their kinds. As such it involves two principles: "that of perceiving and bringing together in one idea the scattered particulars, that one may make clear by definition the particular thing which he wishes to explain"; and "that of dividing things again by classes, where the natural joints are."[25] The former principle involves, for example, uniting the activities of writing stories of the benevolent gods and distributing property in equal shares under the subject of justice, so as to arrive at a definition of justice; the latter principle involves, say, dividing poetry into the sort that provides a sound model and the sort that does not. This uniting and dividing take place in conversation, not in a standard philosophical treatise. The dialogue may begin with what is superficial or seemingly trivial, but it rises from there to what is general or permanent. In the *Republic* Socrates gives an explanation of dialectic as "making the hypotheses [of arguments] not beginnings but really hypotheses—that is, steppingstones and springboards—in order to reach what is free from hypothesis at the beginning of the whole."[26]

> For all the other arts are directed to human opinions and desires, or to generation and composition, or to the care of what is grown or put together. And as for the rest, those that we said do lay hold of something of what is—geometry and the arts following on it—we observe that they do dream about what *is;* but they haven't the capacity to see

it in full awakeness so long as they use hypotheses and, leaving them untouched, are unable to give an account of them. When the beginning is what one doesn't know, and the end and what comes in between are woven out of what isn't known, what contrivance is there for ever turning such an agreement into knowledge? . . . [O]nly the dialectical way of inquiry proceeds in this direction, destroying the hypotheses, to the beginning itself in order to make it secure; . . .[27]

Dialectic is the highest form of reasoning because it alone examines the hypotheses; all other sorts of reasoning, all other arts and sciences, take "what is free from hypothesis," or ultimate first principles, as givens: either they work inductively toward those first principles or they move deductively from them.

Aristotle provides elaboration of what Socrates may mean when he speaks of the ability of dialectic to free us from hypothesis: "For from its own first principles, any given science is incapable of saying anything about them, since the first principles are the first of all; it is instead necessary to proceed by way of the generally accepted opinions about each of them. But this task is either uniquely or especially the province of dialectic. For to it, as the art capable of thorough scrutiny, belongs the path to the ultimate foundations of all paths of knowledge."[28] Thomas Pangle's explanation is worth quoting at length:

All scientific awareness of the world presupposes, and must build from and upon, a prescientific awareness of the world that is the awareness of 'common sense,' the awareness of the world in which we live as perceiving, reasoning, acting, caring, deliberating, reflecting human beings. The commonsense world is dominated or formed by generally accepted opinions. But scientific thinking is continually at risk of forgetting or obscuring its own humble, but inescapable, origins in the 'life world.' Scientific thinking is likely to assume that the movement or ascent from the prescientific to the scientific provides a sufficient criticism of the prescientific. But this assumption is false. The ascent to science can be a rigorous, well-grounded ascent if and only if all the presuppositions inherited from or incorporated into science from the world of common sense have been made fully conscious, and, in addition, have been exposed to a thorough critical scrutiny—a scrutiny that does not presuppose the validity of the ascent, for which the scrutiny alone can provide the foundation. In other words, radical reflection on the prescientific presuppositions of science in general, and of any science in particular, cannot be based on the assumption that the science is valid—for the validity of science, its ground, is what is in question.[29]

The highest knowledge comes from critical, painstaking examination of those presuppositions; that examination comes through dialectic. Dialectic, then, as the source of the highest knowledge, is the master of sciences. Dialectic or philosophy is science, in the highest sense of science. Again, as Leo Strauss observes, philosophy and science were one and the same from the time of Plato even through early modern times, until the nineteenth century.

The questioning that is dialectic requires challenging all of our assumptions about morals, politics, religion—all of our assumptions simply. The result, if we can attain it, is self-knowledge, a full awareness of the principles that guide our mental and physical activity. No longer would we proceed through life ruled by our past experiences; we would have knowledge of the worth of the teachings that shaped our past, knowledge of their strengths as well as weaknesses; hence we would know how to conduct ourselves in the present.

I cannot say here with certainty that Socratic dialectic is entirely undogmatic. As I have said, this is not the place for a full study of Socrates and Plato.[30] So I must make a qualified claim. It is safe to say that Socratic dialectic is undogmatic relative to much of today's philosophizing. Contemporary philosophizing is often quick to presume that human beings simply cannot avoid dogma, or that one's passions will always be master of one's reason. Socratic dialectic makes neither presumption— nor, as far as I know, does it assume the opposite of either of those statements. It aims to challenge all fixed tenets, so that any tenet advanced in an argument or used to justify one's action would be fortified, not merely asserted.

It appears that Socratic dialectic shares a point with historicism. As Pangle explains it in his defense of dialectic, "All human thinking is the thinking, not of 'pure minds,' but of human souls. The human soul is motivated by desire, by love, by need. . . . The world that we know or can know is the world that is of concern to us; it is the world inevitably shaped to some crucial extent by our concerns, or the world of which our concerns are among the preeminent constituents. . . . The questions and the observations are determined by what we value."[31] All human thought is shaped by the context in which it occurs, as historicists claim (contrary to Kant). Historicism goes on to claim, however, that human thought is incapable of transcending its time and place to arrive at anything called permanent knowledge. Socratic dialectic does not subscribe to that tenet. But Socrates does not seem to assume the opposite either: he does not simply presuppose that human thought is capable of entirely transcending its context to arrive at a nonsubjective truth.

The same is true for moral relativism as is true for historicism. Socrates' search for the truth about justice and goodness certainly indicates that he is not a doctrinaire moral relativist. But, as his frequent professions of his ignorance demonstrate, he neither seems to think he is in possession of moral truth nor assumes that absolute moral truth is available to human beings. He does not assume that his search could ever be finished in this life.

Philosophy so understood as dialectic, as a way of life, is not likely to be free of tension. First of all there will be a strain between the philosopher's life of questioning and the statesman's devotion to rule; Socrates clearly predicts that strain when he remarks that the philosopher must be compelled to return to "the cave" to rule.[32] The way of theory and the way of practice do not easily coexist. A specific tension will exist between the life of questioning and obedience to the political law; Socrates makes this clear when he warns that the improper use of dialectic will fill students with lawlessness.[33] The mode of political communication, according to him, is not dialectic but rhetoric.[34] That is less than true science, but still considerably more than rhetoric usually means today. Pangle explains, "The noble art of rhetoric aims to elevate rather than to gratify, to sober rather than to inebriate. The Socratic art of rhetoric seeks to bring into being a mode of civic communication that will awaken and channel popular imagination and fervor without enflaming that imagination and fervor."[35] Rhetoric may communicate true opinion, but it is unrealistic to expect a political community, with its various limitations, to make their public reasoning dialectic. The highest science is not a model for a democratic, or other sort of political, community.

Clearly Dewey disagrees with Socrates on that point; but, in order to understand better their points of disagreement on politics it will be helpful to gauge Dewey's response to Socratic dialectic itself. Dewey describes Socratic dialectic, not as the way of arriving at the truth of things, but as a way of avoiding reality. Human beings have perennially divided existence into supernatural and natural, he says. "There is a long story between the primitive forms of this division of objects of experience and the dialectical imputation to the divine of omnipotence, omniscience, eternity and infinity, in contrast with the attribution to man and experienced nature of finitude, weakness, limitation, struggle and change" (*EN*, 52). Dialectic, then, would falsely reify distinctions, such as that between power and weakness, which can have no more than a functional basis. More precisely, Dewey says, past philosophers and those who copy them "transmute the imaginative perception of the stably good object into a definition and description of true reality in contrast with lower and specious existence, which, being precarious and incomplete, alone involves us in the necessity of choice and active struggle" (*EN*, 51). Thinkers come upon something good, but they are unwilling to act in order to make that good thing last. "Thus it becomes a refuge, an asylum for contemplation, or a theme for dialectical elaboration, instead of an ideal to inspire and guide conduct."

Viewing the history of philosophy, Dewey alleges, "The history of thought seems to me to disclose that the belief in immutable existence is an emotional preference dialectically supported."[36] That, I believe, is the extent of Dewey's defense of historical relativism (to the extent that his allegiance is not totally dogmatic): all attempts to find some immutable truth have been in reality a search for metaphysical comfort; and all claims to have found such truth are mere emotional outpourings dressed up as philosophy.[37]

On Dewey's view, dialectic is not merely a defense mechanism, however. Like philosophy in general, it has a positive place in education of the young, as an aid to science. In chapter 2 we saw Dewey's emphasis on the social aspect of education. Literature and "dialectical methods," he says, are "necessary auxiliary tools" in showing students the intellectual and moral knowledge to be gained from social occupations (*DE*, 325). "But every advance in the influence of the experimental method is sure to aid in outlawing the literary, dialectic, and authoritative methods of forming beliefs which have governed the schools of the past" (*DE*, 349). With dialectic in an auxiliary role, the scientific method is the model of striving for intelligence, whether on the part of scientists or democratic citizens.

The points of political disagreement between Dewey and Socrates follow from their differing views of dialectic. If Dewey is correct about the role of dialectic in the pursuit of knowledge, then Socrates may be incorrect to say that there is no tension between the life of dialectical questioning and the work of the statesman. Recall from *The Public and Its Problems* the key role that Dewey sees for communication in the creation of a "Great Community." Dewey sets no limits on that communication, and he sees it as the task of all citizens, including political leaders, to share with one another the results of their best trial-and-error efforts to solve their moral and social problems. Nor would there be tension between the life of questioning the law and obedience to the law. According to Deweyan pragmatism affirmation of the law is always tentative and comes only after a rigorous questioning of the suitability of the law, a questioning in which all citizens are invited to engage. Again, recall that for Dewey laws are not commands but substitutes of predictability.

Like Socratic dialectic, Deweyan pragmatism does not deny the importance of humans' prescientific awareness of the world. As we saw in the previous chapter, immediate experience is the ground or starting point from which reflective experience emerges. Yet, contrary to common sense, Dewey refuses to call that prescientific awareness knowledge. Leo Strauss observes with reference to what he calls the "decisive example, political science requires clarification of what distinguishes political things from things which are not political; it requires that the question be raised and answered 'what is political?' This question cannot be dealt with scientifically but only dialectically. And dialectical treatment necessarily begins from pre-scientific knowledge and takes it most seriously."[38] Dewey attempts to dignify this prescientific awareness with the term *real;* the awareness of a pain is as real as its scientific demonstration. But science does not settle for what is merely real; it seeks to be able to control what is real for the sake of enhancing the real. If this teaching does not obscure the origins of the scientific in the prescientific, does it nevertheless exaggerate the difference between the prescientific and the scientific?

Another way to put that matter is to ask whether Dewey understands the relation between philosophy and science aright. How can philosophy for Dewey be a way of life when its goal is to help science, and the goal of science is to resolve problematic situations? Some situations are problematic because the totality of factors produces incompleteness, while others are not problematic because the overall result is one of completeness. He emphasizes that the determination of the completeness or lack of such in a situation is not to be left to what we might call the subjective judgment of the person but must respect "the given facts."[39] A problematic aspect of a situation need not be "consciously recognized" as such in order to be problematic.[40] The "conditions in experience" determine what is problematic.[41] When Dewey says that a person need not "recognize" a situation as problematic for it to be so, he does not mean that the person need not have any "feel[ing]" of incompleteness or disharmony. Recall from the previous chapter Dewey's contrast between "having" or "feeling" qualities of things in one's experience and "knowing" about those things or recognizing them (*EN,* 198). The activity that we call "cognition" does not exhaust mental activity in Dewey's scheme. Thus a situation may be problematic without a person's cognition of the problem. In a reply to critics he says that "according to my view a *situation* is problematic prior to any 'grasping' or 'apprehension' whatever, the first act of knowing being to locate *a problem* by selective or analytic discrimination of some of the observable constituents of the total situation."[42] Dewey does not mean "grasping" or "apprehending" to include "feeling" or "having." A person may have a feeling of disharmony, but not until he reflects or knows can he even say exactly what the problem is. When Dewey says that a situation may be problematic without being thought problematic, he comes as close as he ever does to providing an Archimedean point for distinguishing one condition from another—that is, an objective standpoint in the sense of complete independence from human thought or judgment. As we have seen, however, such a standpoint is not to be found on Dewey's view. Human purposes are always a factor in the making of judgments, whether scientific, moral, or any other sort. But we are left with a clear dichotomy between problematic and unproblematic situations; a situation is either one or the other, depending on "conditions in experience." That is to reify a distinction between unproblematic and problematic just as much as Dewey accuses other philosophers of reifying distinctions that are only functional. By Dewey's own antidichotomous standards, then, he exaggerates the difference between unproblematic and problematic situations—the difference, that is, between the prescientific and the scientific. That too makes me doubt the plausibility of the relation between philosophy and science envisioned by Dewey.

Dewey emphasizes his belief that Socratic dialectic hinges on the theory of ideas of the *Republic*. "Unless there were such objective universals, the moral anarchy of subjectivism was inevitable; anything was good or right that seemed to be right or good to an individual at any particular moment."[43] If the validity of Socratic dialectic depends upon a theory of immutable existence, such as the theory of the forms or ideas put forward in the *Republic,* and that theory has not been proved, then indeed Socratic dialectic is highly questionable at best. But it is not at all certain that Socratic dialectic hinges on a claim concerning immutable existence. I am not confident in saying that Socrates believed in the theory of the forms. In the *Republic* he admits to making arguments while in a state of doubt and seeking.[44] In the *Phaedo* he seems to present competing thoughts about the Ideas.[45] It is possible that the ideas or forms serve as the goals of inquiry, not the presuppositions—possible that Socrates and Plato were able to philosophize without commitment to a prior metaphysical or ontological theory.

If Socratic philosophizing is as undogmatic as it appears, its advantages are considerable. First, Dewey's need for an undogmatic philosophy is greater than he admits. As we saw earlier, when he says that he is willing to put his faith in scientific method to the test, he mentions an experimental test. If science is to test science, he is obviously begging the question.

Second, Socratic dialectic might allow us to recognize the inadequacy of postmodernists' dogmatic rejections of philosophical foundations for politics. It would help us to see the problem with Richard Rorty's insouciant rejection of the idea of ahistorical moral truth. It would help us to discern rashness in Cornell West's "left romanticism"—at least the "audacious projection of desires and hopes in the form of regulative emancipatory ideals for which one lives and dies"—by moderating our political demands. Finally, it would help us to do without such assumptions of John Patrick Diggins as "there is no essence" behind our intellectual and physical activity.

Third, it is possible that Socratic dialectic could nonetheless help us to approach the philosophical defense of political institutions without a comprehensive metaphysical scheme. Contrary to Dewey's statement that any political theory lacking grounding in a comprehensive philosophy is only personal preference, we could ask questions such as "what is justice?" without comprehensive knowledge and still move toward finding answers to them. For that to be true, of course, Socratic dialectic would need not to depend on the theory of the forms. Indeed Socrates begins discussing justice at the beginning of the *Republic* and gives a definition of it later, well before he advances the theory of the forms. It is not at all certain that Dewey's insistence on a prior comprehensive philosophy is correct.

Fourth, Socratic dialectic could remind us of the apparently ineradicable tensions among human goods. Alan Ryan calls those tensions "irreducible," and I tend to agree.[46] In particular, Dewey ignores the ever-present tension between the good of the individual human mind and the good of society.

Fifth, Socratic dialectic could contribute toward a rationalist aesthetics, discussed in the previous chapter. It could sort out works of art that are sublime from those that are not (whether the final judgments are public or private). More fundamentally, as Socrates says in the *Republic,* it could make a young person appreciate fine things even before he learns to speak properly and becomes a gentleman.[47]

CONCLUSION

Scholars of various approaches and schools from Alasdair MacIntyre to Leo Strauss to Eric Voegelin have seen in ancient thought the source of something lacking in our lives. The richness of the Greek conception of human life has seemed to them to characterize the human situation in all its contours, an understanding undiminished by whatever intellectual or technological developments arise. In a number of passages Dewey too shows an appreciation for the Greek understanding of human life. Greek thinkers' possession of the ideals of science and reason, and their insistence on making reason not custom the guide to human conduct, were a "permanent" contribution to Western civilization (*QC,* 14). Moreover, liberalism "might be traced back to Greek thought; some of its ideas, especially as to the importance of the free play of intelligence, may be found notably expressed in the funeral oration attributed to Pericles."[48] Perhaps most important for Dewey, despite their scientific limitations, Greek thought was not encumbered by the dichotomy between subjective and objective; thus he calls the Greeks' condition "naive" to suggest a "freshness and directness of approach."[49]

For a variety of reasons of desirability and feasibility, no one suggests that we remold our political institutions and societies to match those of ancient Greece. If claims for advances in political science in the last centuries have at times been exaggerated, still it is hard to deny that in some respects at least they have been advances: a suffrage no longer based on property, extended more widely to men and women; representation; checks and balances, especially an independent judiciary.

As many scholars urge us to rethink the philosophical foundations of our politics, would it be possible to strike a compromise that would enable us to incorporate elements of the Greeks' "freshness and directness of approach," their understanding of human intellectual and moral capabilities, in our political institutions (I mean, generally, liberal democracy)?[50] If it were possible, what would Dewey have to contribute to that compromise?

In separate works, James Nichols Jr. and Thomas Pangle have suggested that Dewey's emphasis on the moral spirit of the scientific method is beneficial to liberal democracies.[51] With postmodernism influencing the lower stages of education in various ways, such an emphasis might be thought welcome, and it might actually be welcome. With the openness to innovation that can accompany the scientific spirit, however, there can come an unnecessary hostility to revealed religion. I wonder whether the benefit gained from the former outweighs the cost of the latter; for it is a central element of Dewey's teaching that science is *the* way for students to approach truth. Perhaps the cost in lower education would be lessened by a greater emphasis on questioning science itself in higher education.

What I find particularly constructive in Dewey's thought for the aforementioned compromise is his educational emphasis on interest and discipline as related terms (*DE,* chap. 10). His insistence on starting with children's interests in developing school activities is a significant improvement on the traditional method of rote memorization, which treats school subjects as if they really were Platonic forms waiting to be grasped.

> To have an interest is to take things as entering into . . . a continuously developing situation, instead of taking them in isolation. The time

difference between the given incomplete state of affairs and the desired fulfillment exacts effort in transformation; it demands continuity of attention and endurance. This attitude is what is practically meant by will. Discipline or development of power of continuous attention is its fruit.

The significance of this doctrine for the theory of education is twofold. On the one hand it protects us from the notion that mind and mental states are something complete in themselves, which then happen to be applied to some ready-made objects and topics so that knowledge results. It shows that mind and intelligent or purposeful engagement in a course of action into which things enter are identical. . . . On the other side, it protects us from the notion that subject matter on its side is something isolated and independent. (*DE,* 144–45)

If Socratic philosophy is as nonabsolutist as some scholars suggest, Dewey's reliance on interest as a starting point and discipline as aim fits well with it (if we pass over his failure to emphasize teaching reading at the earliest possible age).[52]

What is more problematic for an ancient-modern compromise is Dewey's constant emphasis that everything in education be done with a view toward the social. One might well ask, would Dewey's educational principles, if followed to the letter, produce a John Dewey? Again I agree here with Ryan, who charged Dewey with failing to consider his own habits in writing about philosophy and education. "His emphasis on practical, engaged thought understated the need for impractical and disengaged thinking."[53] He understood that he was mainly a solitary worker—that he needed space free from direct public or social involvement to think—but he did not make allowance for that solitude in others.[54]

That neglect casts doubt on Dewey's psychological theory (further doubt than what I indicated in chapter 2). Dewey dislikes the word "reason" to describe the human ability to think, because it indicates too much a separate faculty that must be located somewhere in the mind. He much prefers the term "intelligence," which "has something to do" (*RP,* 134–35). But intelligence, according to Dewey, turns out to be nothing other than a collection of social habits: "[c]oncrete habits do all the perceiving, recognizing, imagining, recalling, judging, conceiving and reasoning that is done" (*HNC,* 124). It seems impossible, on this view, that a human being could possess a unique (divinely inspired?) spark or stuff that makes him or her a unique person. Rather the uniqueness of intelligence must be *wholly* accounted for by a different grouping of habits. I do not see how this theory can explain the master strokes of genius that produced at least some (I would actually say most or all) of the literary, artistic, philosophical, scientific, or technological breakthroughs in human history. Although I do not think that intelligence can be satisfactorily defined as a collection of habits, I stop short of appealing to a faculty psychology or any definite psychological theory. But it is highly doubtful that reason is the simple equivalent of social intelligence.

While I agree with Ryan's criticisms of Dewey's neglect of the private world, I heartily disagree with certain of his educational formulations. Calling for a more "intellectualist" schooling, Ryan says that education for some people should focus on "the promotion of sheer cleverness and the inculcation of enough factual and theoretical raw material for a developing student to employ his cleverness on."[55] Dewey was correct to insist on a moral purpose running throughout the child's education. On that point he and Aristotle (who argues that cleverness needs a noble aim in order to be praiseworthy), for one, are in agreement.[56] It does not follow, however, that a more intellectualist schooling would not be welcome. We can restate Ryan's goal as intellectual activity for its own sake, with no practical goal in mind. This is part of the Socratic dialectic and should be welcomed in higher education, but I doubt whether Ryan captures its meaning when he champions "the quirky, idiosyncratic, and self-centered."[57] Here again I think Dewey— despite his lack of attention to private life—is more generally correct to hold that higher intellectual activity should arise out of serious engagement with daily concerns. Otherwise we are all too likely to see a growing number of aimless youth in America, who care about no one or nothing but themselves, and whose lives seem to them trivial because they are preoccupied with trivia, or "the quirky."

I do not want to give the impression that I would simply characterize John Dewey as closed-minded—far from it. His writings display a remarkable open-mindedness on many subjects, from economics to art. To a great extent he did take the experimental method to heart.

When we ask about the philosophical roots of Dewey's political thought, however, it has been my contention that we do find a questionable absolutism: his commitments to historical relativism and scientific method. When he argues both that scientific method discloses nature over time and that the ideas of political theorists are inherently limited by their time and place, we see that he has not faced squarely the issue of historicism.

Dewey does us a service when he rejects the inflexible character of past philosophy. The heart of the matter for him is that philosophy must learn from science not to assume a realm of fixed ideals; philosophy must learn to be experimental or tentative. The questions that I would ask are, "If philosophy goes to modern science to learn that lesson, can it do any better than to have *faith in* science?" "Will it not be likely to acquire the baggage of dogmatic, metaphysical materialism?"

If instead philosophy goes to Socratic dialectic to learn to be tentative, will it have arrived at an undogmatic starting point? It behooves us to study Socratic philosophy carefully in order to determine whether such an alternative is viable.

NOTES

1. John Dewey, "Experience, Knowledge, and Value: A Rejoinder," in L14:64; see also 86–88. See also John Dewey, "The Unity of the Human Being" (1939), in L14:331; "The Field of 'Value' " (1949), in L16:343–57.

2. W. H. Sheldon, "Critique of Naturalism," *Journal of Philosophy* 42 (10 May 1945): 252–70.

3. John Dewey (with Sidney Hook and Ernest Nagel), "Are Naturalists Materialists?" (1945), in L15 (1989): 116. Hook and Nagel wrote most of this essay, but Dewey did sign his name to the whole piece.

4. Ibid., 123.

5. For one of the latest critiques of Dewey finding an all-pervasive concern for promoting democracy in his thought, see Peter Berkowitz, "The Religion of Democracy," *Public Interest* 132 (winter 1996): 133–39.

6. See Leo Strauss, *Natural Right and History* (Chicago: University of Chicago Press, 1953), 78–79. See also Leo Strauss, "Progress or Return? The Contemporary Crisis in Western Civilization," in *An Introduction to Political Philosophy: Ten Essays by Leo Strauss,* ed. Hilail Gildin (Detroit: Wayne State University Press, 1989), 266.

7. Dewey and Bentley, *Philosophical Correspondence,* 629.

8. John Dewey, "The Future of Liberalism" (1935), in L11:290–92. See

also John Dewey, "Introduction to *Problems of Men:* The Problems of Men and the Present State of Philosophy" (1946), in L15:162–63.

9. John Dewey, *German Philosophy and Politics* (1915), in M8 (1979): 201.

10. John Dewey, "Pragmatic America" (1922), in M13:308–9.

11. George Santayana, "Dewey's Naturalistic Metaphysics," *Journal of Philosophy* 22 (1925): 687.

12. Dewey, " 'Half-Hearted Naturalism,' " 74.

13. Dewey, "Experience, Knowledge and Value," 79–80.

14. John Dewey, *A Common Faith* (1934), in L9:6.

15. Ibid., 11.

16. Ibid., 12.

17. Ibid., 29, 36.

18. I am grateful to Thomas Pangle for suggesting the comparison between Dewey and Fish.

19. Stanley Fish, "Liberalism Doesn't Exist," 1987 *Duke Law Journal* 997. For Carter's article see "Evolutionism, Creationism, and Treating Religion as a Hobby," 1987 *Duke Law Journal* 977–96.

20. Ibid., 1000.

21. Ibid., 998.

22. Ibid., 1000.

23. John Rawls, *Political Liberalism* (New York: Columbia University Press, 1993), 192.

24. As I finish this manuscript a book has just been published that also deals with both Deweyan pragmatism and philosophy as a way of life: Richard Shusterman, *Practicing Philosophy: Pragmatism and the Philosophical Life* (New York: Routledge, 1997). I have not had a chance to read the entire book, but I strongly disagree with Shusterman's claim that ancient political philosophy is "far too dated" to be helpful to us today (7).

25. Plato, *Phaedrus,* trans. Harold North Fowler (Cambridge: Harvard University Press, 1914), 533 at 265d, 535 at 265e.

26. Plato, *Republic,* 2d ed., trans. Allan Bloom (New York: Basic Books, 1991), 191 at 511b.

27. Ibid., 212 at 533b-c.

28. Aristotle, *Topics,* 101a37-b4, trans. Pangle in *Ennobling of Democracy,* 185. My understanding of Socratic philosophy is indebted to Pangle's account.

29. Pangle, *Ennobling of Democracy,* 185–86.

30. There are detailed studies of Socrates claiming that he does offer an undogmatic defense of rationalism. See, e.g., Peter J. Ahrensdorf, *The Death of Socrates and the Life of Philosophy* (Albany: State University of New York Press, 1995); Paul Stern, *Socratic Rationalism and Political Philosophy* (Albany: State University of New York Press, 1993). Also on the undogmatism of Socrates see Strauss, "Progress or Return?" 300.

31. Pangle, *Ennobling of Democracy*, 186–87.

32. Plato, *Republic*, 519c–520a.

33. Ibid., 537e; see also 539b–c.

34. See Plato, *Gorgias*, 471.

35. Pangle, *Ennobling of Democracy*, 130.

36. John Dewey, "In Reply to Some Criticisms" (1930), in L5:213.

37. Here is one criticism Dewey makes of Greek philosophy: "Without Greek religion, Greek art, Greek civic life, their [i.e., Plato's and Aristotle's] philosophy would have been impossible; while the effect of that science upon which the philosophers most prided themselves turns out to have been superficial and negligible" (*RP*, 90).

38. Leo Strauss, *What is Political Philosophy? and Other Studies* (Chicago: University of Chicago Press, 1959), 24–25.

39. John Dewey, "The Logic of Judgments of Practice" (1915), in M8:20.

40. Dewey, contributions to *A Cyclopedia of Education*, vols. 3–5, 330.

41. Ibid., 331.

42. Dewey, "Experience, Knowledge, and Value," 70.

43. Dewey, contributions to *A Cyclopedia of Education*, vols. 3–5, 229.

44. Plato, *Republic*, 450c–451a.

45. For an examination of this see Stern, *Socratic Rationalism*, especially chap. 4.

46. Ryan, *Dewey and American Liberalism*, 328.

47. Plato, *Republic*, 401d–402a.

48. Dewey, *Liberalism and Social Action*, 6.

49. John Dewey, "The Objectivism-Subjectivism of Modern Philosophy" (1941), in L14:192.

50. Thomas Pangle makes such a suggestion; see introduction, *Ennobling of Democracy*, 1–15.

51. Nichols, "Pragmatism and the U.S. Constitution"; Pangle, *Ennobling of Democracy*.

52. I partially agree with the criticism made by Richard Hofstadter, *Anti-Intellectualism in American Life* (New York: Vintage, 1963), who charges Dewey's educational theory with promoting anti-intellectualism. Yet, as Westbrook observes, Dewey does prescribe subjects to be taught more than Hofstadter realizes. Westbrook, *Dewey and American Democracy*, 104.

53. Ryan, *Dewey and American Liberalism*, 121.

54. I do not mean to slight Dewey's numerous public activities, only to say that his primary work was academic philosophy.

55. Ryan, *Dewey and American Liberalism*, 347.

56. Aristotle, *Nicomachean Ethics*, 1144a24–b1.

57. Ryan, *Dewey and American Liberalism*, 368.

BIBLIOGRAPHY

Ahrensdorf, Peter J. *The Death of Socrates and the Life of Philosophy.* Albany: State University of New York Press, 1995.

Alexander, Thomas M. "Richard Rorty and Dewey's Metaphysics of Experience." *Southwest Philosophical Studies* 5 (1980): 24–35.

———. *John Dewey's Theory of Art, Experience, and Nature: The Horizons of Feeling.* Albany: State University of New York Press, 1987.

Anderson, Charles. *Pragmatic Liberalism.* Chicago: University of Chicago Press, 1990.

Aristotle. *Nicomachean Ethics.*

———. *Politics.*

Berkowitz, Peter. "The Religion of Democracy." *Public Interest* 132 (winter 1996): 133–39.

Berlin, Sir Isaiah. *Two Concepts of Liberty.* Oxford: Oxford University Press, Clarendon Press, 1958.

Bernstein, Richard J. "Philosophy in the Conversation of Mankind." *Review of Metaphysics* 33 (1980): 745–75.

———. *Beyond Objectivism and Relativism: Science, Hermeneutics, and Praxis.* Oxford: Basil Blackwell, 1983.

———. "One Step Forward, Two Steps Backward: Richard Rorty on Liberal Democracy and Philosophy." *Political Theory* 15 (November 1987): 538–63.

Bloom, Allan. *The Closing of the American Mind.* New York: Simon and Schuster, 1987.

Boisvert, Raymond D. *Dewey's Metaphysics.* New York: Fordham University Press, 1988.

Brodsky, Garry. "Rorty's Interpretation of Pragmatism." *Transactions of the Charles S. Peirce Society* 18 (1982): 311–37.

Burke, Edmund. *A Philosophical Enquiry into the Origin of our Ideas of the Sublime and Beautiful.* Edited by James T. Boulton. London: Routledge and Kegan Paul, 1958 (1757).

157

Campbell, James. "Rorty's Use of Dewey." *Southern Journal of Philosophy* 22 (summer 1984): 175–88.

Ceaser, James W. *Liberal Democracy and Political Science.* Baltimore: Johns Hopkins University Press, 1990.

Cunningham, Craig A. Electronic mail on John Dewey discussion list (dewey-l@postoffice.cso.uiuc.edu), "continuity [and discontinuity]," 15 February 1996.

Damico, Alfonso J. *Individuality and Community: The Social and Political Thought of John Dewey.* Gainesville: University Presses of Florida, 1978.

Dewey, John. *The Early Works, 1882–1898.* 5 vols. Edited by Jo Ann Boydston. Carbondale: Southern Illinois University Press, 1969–75.

————. *The Middle Works, 1899–1924.* 15 vols. Edited by Jo Ann Boydston. Carbondale: Southern Illinois University Press, 1976–83. (Abbreviated elsewhere in this bibliography as M followed by volume number and date of publication in parentheses.)

————. *The Later Works, 1925–1953.* 17 vols. Edited by Jo Ann Boydston. Carbondale: Southern Illinois University Press, 1981–90. (Abbreviated elsewhere in this bibliography as L followed by volume number and date of publication in parentheses.)

Dewey, John, and Arthur F. Bentley. *John Dewey and Arthur F. Bentley: A Philosophical Correspondence, 1932–1951.* Edited by Sidney Ratner and Jules Altman. New Brunswick, N.J.: Rutgers University Press, 1964.

Diggins, John Patrick. *The Promise of Pragmatism: Modernism and the Crisis of Knowledge and Authority.* Chicago: University of Chicago Press, 1994.

Eames, S. Morris. *Pragmatic Naturalism: An Introduction.* Carbondale: Southern Illinois University Press, 1977.

Eisenberg, Avigail I. *Reconstructing Political Pluralism.* Albany: State University of New York Press, 1995.

Fish, Stanley. "Liberalism Doesn't Exist." *Duke Law Journal* (December 1987): 997–1001.

Gavin, William J., ed. *Context over Foundation: Dewey and Marx.* Sovietica Series, vol. 52. Dordrecht, Holland: D. Reidel, 1988.

Hassner, Pierre. "Georg W. F. Hegel." Translated by Allan Bloom. In *History of Political Philosophy,* 3d ed., edited by Leo Strauss and Joseph Cropsey. Chicago: University of Chicago Press, 1987.

Hegel, Georg W. F. *Philosophy of Right.* Translated by T. M. Knox. London: Oxford University Press, 1952.

Hobbes, Thomas. *Leviathan.*

Hofstadter, Richard. *Anti-Intellectualism in American Life.* New York: Vintage, 1963.

Holmes, Stephen. "Practically Wisdom." *New Republic,* 11 March 1996, 40–46.

Hook, Sidney. *Pragmatism and the Tragic Sense of Life.* New York: Basic Books, 1974.

————. "Introduction." In Dewey, M9 (1980).

————. "Introduction." In Dewey, L1 (1981).

Horwitz, Robert. "John Dewey." In *History of Political Philosophy,* edited by Leo Strauss and Joseph Cropsey. 3d ed. Chicago: University of Chicago Press, 1987.

Klyce, Scudder. Papers. John Dewey to Scudder Klyce, 21 October 1927. General Correspondence: John Dewey: Manuscript Division, Library of Congress. Washington, D.C.

Lamont, Corliss. "New Light on Dewey's *Common Faith.*" *Journal of Philosophy* 58 (1961): 21–28.

Lavine, T. Z. "Introduction." In Dewey, L16 (1989).

Lawler, Peter. "Pragmatism, Existentialism, and the Crisis in American Political Thought." In *John Dewey: Critical Assessments,* vol. 2, edited by J. E. Tiles. London: Routledge, 1992.

Levi, Isaac. "Escape from Boredom: Edification According to Rorty." *Canadian Journal of Philosophy* 11 (December 1981): 589–602.

Lippmann, Walter. *The Phantom Public.* New York: Macmillan, 1925.

Locke, John. *A Letter Concerning Toleration.*

————. *Some Thoughts Concerning Education.*

————. *Two Treatises of Government.* Edited by Peter Laslett. Cambridge: Cambridge University Press, 1988.

Longinus. *On Great Writing (On the Sublime).* Translated by G. M. A. Grube. Indianapolis: Hackett, 1991.

Lyotard, Jean-Francois. *The Postmodern Condition: A Report on Knowledge.* Translated by Geoff Bennington and Brian Massumi. Minneapolis: University of Minnesota Press, 1984.

————. "The Sublime and the Avant-Garde." Translated by Lisa Liebmann. In *The Lyotard Reader,* rev. ed., edited by Andrew Benjamin. Oxford: Blackwell, 1989.

MacIntyre, Alasdair. *After Virtue.* 2d ed. Notre Dame, Ind.: University of Notre Dame Press, 1984.

Mansfield, Harvey C. "Democracy and the Great Books." *New Republic,* 4 April 1988, 33–37.

————. "Dewey, All-out Democrat." *Times Literary Supplement,* 24 January 1992, 26.

————. "Self-Interest Rightly Understood." *Political Theory* 23 (February 1995): 48–66.

————. "Manliness and Liberalism." Unpublished paper.

Marx, Karl. *On the Jewish Question.*

Marx, Karl, and Friedrich Engels. *Manifesto of the Communist Party.*

Metz, Joseph G. "Democracy and the Scientific Method in the Philosophy of John Dewey." *Review of Politics* 31 (April 1969): 242–62.

Mill, John Stuart. *Utilitarianism.* Edited by George Sher. Indianapolis: Hackett, 1979 (1861).

Nagel, Ernest. "Introduction" to Dewey, L12 (1986).

Nielsen, Kai. "Scientism, Pragmatism, and the Fate of Philosophy." *Inquiry* 29 (1986): 277–304.

Nietzsche, Friedrich. *Beyond Good and Evil.*

———. *Ecce Homo.*

Nichols, James H., Jr. "Pragmatism and the U.S. Constitution." In *Confronting the Constitution,* edited by Allan Bloom. Washington, D.C.: AEI Press, 1990.

Pangle, Thomas L. *The Ennobling of Democracy: The Challenge of the Postmodern Age.* Baltimore: Johns Hopkins University Press, 1992.

Plato. *Gorgias.*

———. *Phaedrus.* Translated by Harold North Fowler. Cambridge: Harvard University Press, 1914.

———. *Republic.* 2d ed. Translated by Allan Bloom. New York: Basic Books, 1991.

Putnam, Hilary. *Reason, Truth and History.* Cambridge: Cambridge University Press, 1981.

———. "A Reconsideration of Deweyan Democracy." In *Pragmatism in Law and Society,* edited by Michael Brint and William Weaver. Boulder, Colo.: Westview, 1991.

———. *Renewing Philosophy.* Cambridge: Harvard University Press, 1992.

———. *Pragmatism.* Oxford: Blackwell, 1995.

Rawls, John. *A Theory of Justice.* Cambridge: Harvard University Press, Belknap Press, 1971.

———. *Political Liberalism.* New York: Columbia University Press, 1993.

Rockefeller, Steven C. *John Dewey: Religious Faith and Democratic Humanism.* New York: Columbia University Press, 1991.

Rorty, Richard. *Philosophy and the Mirror of Nature.* Princeton: Princeton University Press, 1979.

———. "Postmodernist Bourgeois Liberalism." In *Hermeneutics and Praxis,* edited by Robert Hollinger. Notre Dame, Ind.: University of Notre Dame Press, 1985.

———. "Thugs and Theorists: A Reply to Bernstein." *Political Theory* 15 (November 1987): 564–80.

———. "The Priority of Democracy to Philosophy." In *The Virginia Statute for Religious Freedom: Its Evolution and Consequences in American History,* edited by Merrill D. Peterson and Robert C. Vaughan. Cambridge: Cambridge University Press, 1988.

————. *Contingency, Irony, and Solidarity.* Cambridge: Cambridge University Press, 1989.

————. *Objectivity, Relativism, and Truth.* Philosophical Papers, vol. 1. Cambridge: Cambridge University Press, 1991.

————. "For a More Banal Politics." *Harper's Magazine,* May 1992, 16–21.

————. "Something to Steer By." Review of *John Dewey and the High Tide of American Liberalism,* by Alan Ryan. *London Review of Books,* 20 June 1996, 7–8.

Rousseau, Jean-Jacques. *Discourse on Political Economy.* In *The Collected Writings of Rousseau,* vol. 3, edited by Roger D. Masters and Christopher Kelly. Translated by Judith R. Bush, Roger D. Masters, Christopher Kelly, and Terence Marshall. Hanover, N.H.: University Press of New England, 1992.

Ryan, Alan. *John Dewey and the High Tide of American Liberalism.* New York: Norton, 1995.

Sandel, Michael J. *Liberalism and the Limits of Justice.* Cambridge: Cambridge University Press, 1982.

————. "Morality and the Liberal Ideal." *New Republic,* 7 May 1984, 15–17.

————. *Democracy's Discontent: America in Search of a Public Philosophy.* Cambridge: Harvard University Press, 1996.

————. "Dewey Rides Again." *New York Review of Books,* 9 May 1996, 35–38.

Santayana, George. "Dewey's Naturalistic Metaphysics." *Journal of Philosophy* 22 (1925): 673–88.

Schwarzenbach, Sibyl A. "Rawls, Hegel, and Communitarianism." *Political Theory* 19 (November 1991): 539–71.

Sharpe, Anne S., ed. *Index to the Collected Works of John Dewey, 1882–1953.* Carbondale: Southern Illinois University Press, 1991.

Sheldon, W. H. "Critique of Naturalism." *Journal of Philosophy* 42 (10 May 1945): 252–70.

Shusterman, Richard. *Practicing Philosophy: Pragmatism and the Philosophical Life.* New York: Routledge, 1997.

Sleeper, R. W. "Rorty's Pragmatism: Afloat in Neurath's Boat, But Why Adrift?" *Transactions of the Charles S. Peirce Society* 21 (1985): 9–20.

————. *The Necessity of Pragmatism: John Dewey's Conception of Philosophy.* New Haven, Conn.: Yale University Press, 1986.

————. "John Dewey and the Founding Fathers." In *Values and Value Theory in Twentieth-Century America: Essays in Honor of Elizabeth Flower,* edited by Murray G. Murphey and Ivar Berg. Philadelphia: Temple University Press, 1988.

Smith, John. *Purpose and Thought: The Meaning of Pragmatism.* Chicago: University of Chicago Press, 1978.

Steiner, David M. "The Possibility of Paideia: Democratic Education in Jean-Jacques Rousseau and John Dewey." Ph.D. diss., Harvard University, 1989.

————. *Rethinking Democratic Education: The Politics of Reform*. Baltimore: Johns Hopkins University Press, 1994.

Stern, Paul. *Socratic Rationalism and Political Philosophy*. Albany: State University of New York Press, 1993.

Strauss, Leo. *The Political Philosophy of Hobbes: Its Basis and Its Genesis*. Translated by Elsa M. Sinclair. Chicago: University of Chicago Press, 1952 (1936).

————. *Natural Right and History*. Chicago: University of Chicago Press, 1953.

————. *What Is Political Philosophy? and Other Studies*. Chicago: University of Chicago Press, 1959.

————. *Studies in Platonic Political Philosophy*. Chicago: University of Chicago Press, 1983.

————. *An Introduction to Political Philosophy: Ten Essays by Leo Strauss*. Edited by Hilail Gildin. Detroit: Wayne State University Press, 1989.

Thayer, H. S. *Meaning and Action: A Critical History of Pragmatism*. 2d ed. Indianapolis: Hackett, 1981.

Tiles, J. E. *Dewey*. London: Routledge, 1988.

Tocqueville, Alexis de. *Democracy in America*. Edited by J. P. Mayer. Translated by George Lawrence. Garden City, N.Y.: Anchor, 1969.

Walzer, Michael. *Spheres of Justice*. New York: Basic Books, 1983.

Welchman, Jennifer. *Dewey's Ethical Thought*. Ithaca: Cornell University Press, 1995.

West, Cornel. *The American Evasion of Philosophy: A Genealogy of Pragmatism*. Madison: University of Wisconsin Press, 1989.

————. "The Limits of Neopragmatism." In *Pragmatism in Law and Society,* edited by Michael Brint and William Weaver. Boulder, Colo.: Westview, 1991.

Westbrook, Robert B. *John Dewey and American Democracy*. Ithaca: Cornell University Press, 1991.

INDEX

Adams, Henry, 10
aesthetic experience. *See* experience, aesthetic
aesthetics, 22, 91, chap. 4 passim, 125; rationalist, 119–21, 125, 149
Alexander, Thomas, 71, 111
analytic philosophy. *See* philosophy, analytic
Anderson, Charles, 1, 9–10, 12, 13–15
Aquinas, Thomas, 111
Aristotle, 87, 110, 132, 142, 152
art, 22, 69, 100–101, 103–4, 107–8, 110, 111, 114, 115, 126, 129, 149, 152; Aristotle on, 142; Dewey's definition of, 101; Kant on, 112; rhetoric as, 144; and science, 99, 100, 105, 106–7, 109, 116; Socrates on, 141–42

Bentham, Jeremy, 51
Bentley, Arthur F., 21, 85, 86, 87
Bernstein, Richard, 21, 63
Bloom, Allan, 117
Brandeis, Louis D., 37, 67
Burke, Edmund, 100, 108, 110, 112, 118, 120

Carter, Stephen, 138
character, 43, 54–55, 57, 73

Christianity, 6–7, 84–85, 136
communication, 43, 46, 54–55, 78–79, 82, 85, 115; rhetoric as, 144, 146
communitarianism, 16, 45–47
community, 16, 19, 30, 31, 138, 146; Rorty on, 4, 88; scientific, 43. *See also* fraternity
continuity, 16, 20, 68–73, 78–80, 84–85, 86, 87, 89–90, 150–51; Dewey's arguments for, 80–82
creativity, 22, 99–100, 108, 113, 114–21

Damico, Alfonso, 16, 18
Declaration of Independence, 1, 10, 12, 20, 37, 88, 117
democracy, 16, 17, 19, 36, 41, 46, 51, 57, 58, 99, 100, 114, 115, 117, 119, 121; compared to science, 42–44, 116; industrial, 40; as moral ideal, 64–67, 77; philosophical justification of, 3–12, 18, 20, chap. 3 passim
Derrida, Jacques, 5, 7, 63, 108, 109
dialectic, 125, 141–44, 148–49, 152, 153; Dewey's view of, 144–48
Diderot, Denis, 110
Diggins, John Patrick, 1, 10–12, 148

dogmatism, 6–7, 88, 125, 128, 135–41, 143, 145, 148

Eames, S. Morris, 69
education, 19, 20–21, 35, 36, 42–43, 52, 54, 56, 65, 87, 107, 114, 128, 145, 150–52; civic, 22, 100, 114–21; philosophy as theory of, 130, 131
Ellis, Albert, 53
Emerson, Ralph Waldo, 6
emotion, 36, 68, 81, 103–4, 117
enthusiasm, 112–13, 118, 121
equality, 32, 79
experience, 2, 3, 17, 64, 67, 68–70, 76, 86, 90, 91, 101, 109, 112, 130–31, 133, 134, 135, 137, 145, 147; aesthetic, 3, 9, 99, 102–3, 104, 106, 107, 108, 109–10, 111, 112–13, 115, 130, 133, 135, 137; consummatory, 9, 111; immediate, 100, 101–2, 104, 146; reflective, 104–6, 108, 146; religious, 136–37

feeling, vs. thinking, 101–2, 103, 104–5, 115, 116, 117, 147
Fish, Stanley, 137–39
forms, Platonic theory of, 5, 103, 148, 149, 150
foundationalism. *See* democracy, philosophical justification of
fraternity, 79. *See also* community
freedom. *See* liberty

generic traits of existence, 69, 72, 80, 88, 89, 133
growth, 45, 65–67, 69, 70–71, 77, 133, 137, 139. *See also* continuity

habit, 42, 43, 44, 52, 54, 73, 81, 83, 151–52

Hartz, Louis, 9
Hassner, Pierre, 33
Hegel, Georg W. F., 22, 33, 35, 38, 136
Heidegger, Martin, 4, 11, 18, 63
historicism, 6, 11, 113, 143–44, 153
Hobbes, Thomas, 13, 33, 139
Hofstadter, Richard, 19
Holmes, Oliver Wendell, 37, 67
Holmes, Stephen, 90
Hook, Sidney, 21, 83–84, 89–90
human nature, 34, 35, 44, 67–68, 71, 72–73, 77, 79, 84, 99, 135

individualism, 33, 35–38, 44, 57, 79; Tocqueville's conception of, 56, 117
individuality, 35–39, 44–45, 55, 79
intensification, 110–13, 118–19, 120

James, William, 7
Jefferson, Thomas, 1, 6, 10, 12, 88

Kant, Immanuel, 7, 100, 108, 112, 113, 139, 144
Keats, John, 110

Laslett, Peter, 34
Lavine, T. Z., 85–86
law, 36, 53, 55–56, 69, 127–28, 144, 146; natural, 20, 34, 63, 74, 84, 88, 111
liberalism, 15–16, 17, chap. 2 passim, 67, 79, 84, 113, 116, 118, 120–21, 134, 137, 139–40, 149–50; Anderson on, 9–10, 13–15; Fish on, 137–39; Rorty on, 4, 12–13; Ryan on, 19
liberty, 32–33, 37, 52, 55–57, 69, 113, 134
Lippmann, Walter, 29

Locke, John, 33–35, 37–39, 47, 57, 120, 139
Longinus, 109, 118–19
Lyotard, Jean-Francois, 3, 100, 108, 110–13, 118, 120

MacIntyre, Alasdair, 45, 149
Maine, Sir Henry, 65
majority, 31, 48, 55; basis of power of, 48, 50–52; effects of power of, 48–50, 52–54; tyranny of, 47–48, 116, 120–21
Mansfield, Harvey C., 56
Marx, Karl, or Marxism, 6, 38, 44, 65, 114
materialism, 126–28, 140, 153
metaphysics, 5, 7, 9, 45, 126–28, 131, 132, 140, 145, 148, 153; Dewey's, 18, 20, 33, 58, 68–73, 79–82, 84–91, 133–34
Mill, John Stuart, 12, 64, 75, 139

Nagel, Ernest, 90
natural law. *See* law, natural
natural rights. *See* rights, natural
naturalism, 20, 69–71, 73, 88, 89, 126–28, 135
nature, 7, 17, 18, 68–71, 73, 75, 76, 80, 88, 89, 101, 130, 132, 133, 137, 145, 153
Nichols, James Jr., 20, 150
Nietzsche, Friedrich, 11, 13, 21, 63, 88, 89, 99, 117
Nozick, Robert, 45

Pangle, Thomas, 110, 119, 121, 142–44, 150
Pericles, 149
philosophy, 5, 11, 17, 18, 22, 85–86, 91, 121, 125, 140–44, 148–53; an-alytic, 3, 20, 88–89; Dewey's conception of, 69, 125–36, 144–48
Plato, 21, 41, 103, 107–8, 119, 131, 132, 141, 143, 148
postmodernism, 3, 7, 10–12, 18, 63, 88, 100, 108–14, 116–17, 120
pragmatism, Deweyan, 1–3, 18, 20, 22, 73, 135, 136, 146
private. *See* public, and private
public, a or the, 32–48, 51–54, 139; and private, 5, 12–16, 30–32, 36–37, 57, 83, 108–9, 116
Putnam, Hilary, 1, 7–9, 12, 87–88

quality, 68, 69, 74, 89, 101–2, 104, 105, 110, 127, 128–29, 133, 147

rationalist aesthetics. *See* aesthetics, rationalist
Rawls, John, 45, 47, 139
reality. *See* truth, and reality
relativism, 4, 66, 87; historical, 37, 113, 116–18, 119–20, 134, 135, 139, 145, 153; moral, 8–9, 144
religion, revealed, 125, 135–40, 150. *See also* Christianity
rights, natural, 10, 12, 34, 37, 67, 84, 120
Rockefeller, Steven, 17
Rorty, Richard, 1, 3–5, 6, 7, 9, 11, 12–13, 17–18, 21, 63, 88, 106, 148; contrasted with Dewey, 22, 82–83, 88, 91, 100
Rousseau, Jean-Jacques, 6, 38, 40
Ryan, Alan, 18–20, 90, 149, 151–52

Sandel, Michael, 16, 45–47
Santayana, George, 135
science, 16, 54, 56, 73–76, 77, 80, 89, 90, 99–100, 101–8, 112–13, 114–15, 116–17, 136–37, 139, 140,

142–43, 144, 148, 149, 150, 153;
  Dewey's conception of, 7–8, 10,
  42–43, 74, 109
science, compared to democracy. *See*
  democracy, compared to science
science, relation to philosophy. *See*
  philosophy, Dewey's conception of
self-interest, and public spirit, 56–57
Shakespeare, William, 110
Sheldon, W. H., 127
situation, 68, 77–78, 82, 85, 116,
  128–29, 137, 150; problematic,
  2–3, 99, 136, 146–47
Sleeper, R. W., 85
Smith, John E., 2, 76
Socrates, 22, 107, 125, 131, 132, 141–
  46, 148–49, 151, 152, 153
soul, Dewey's conception of, 128–29
state, Dewey's conception of, 30–33,
  36, 41, 47–48, 51, 52, 53, 137,
  139–40
Steiner, David, 20, 87–88
Strauss, Leo, 143, 146, 149
sublimation, 52–53
sublime, 5, 108, 109–12, 118–21, 125,
  126, 149

Thayer, H. S., 2, 71
thinking. *See* feeling, vs. thinking
Tiles, J. E., 107
Tocqueville, Alexis de, 47, 48–50, 52,
  55–57, 119
transaction, 30, 31, 39–40, 41, 68, 74,
  76, 77, 82, 86–87, 99, 113
truth, 4, 6–8, 11–12, 43, 76, 88, 108,
  119–20, 125, 127, 134, 135, 136–
  37, 138, 139, 144, 145, 148, 150;
  and reality, 105, 116–17; correspondence theory of, 2–3, 73, 76,
  116
Tufts, James H., 41, 64
tyranny of the majority. *See* majority,
  tyranny of

Unger, Roberto, 6, 15

Voegelin, Eric, 149

West, Cornel, 1, 5–7, 12, 15, 148
Westbrook, Robert, 17–18
Wittgenstein, Ludwig, 4, 5, 18, 63

ABOUT THE AUTHOR

David Fott is associate professor of political science at the University of Nevada, Las Vegas, where he teaches political theory and American political thought. He received his B.A., *summa cum laude,* from Vanderbilt University and his Ph.D. from Harvard University. He is author of articles on American presidential power and Jane Austen as well as Dewey.